THE BIG BOOK OF

Noodles

THE BIG BOOK OF

Noodles

Over 100 delicious recipes from China, Japan, and Southeast Asia

VATCHARIN BHUMICHITR

Food Photography by Will Heap

Location Photography by Somchai Phongphaisarnkit

Kyle Books

Published in 2011 by Kyle Books,
an imprint of Kyle Cathie Ltd.
www.kylebooks.com

Distributed by National Book Network
4501 Forbes Blvd., Suite 200
Lanham, MD 20706
Phone: (800) 462-6420
Fax: (301) 429-5746
custserv@nbnbooks.com

First published in Great Britain in 2010 by
Kyle Cathie Limited
www.kylecathie.com

ISBN 978 1 906868 14 7

Library of Congress Control Number: 2011920340

10 9 8 7 6 5 4 3 2 1

Text copyright © 2010 by Vatcharin Bumichitr
Design © 2010 by Kyle Cathie Limited
Food photographs © 2010 by Will Heap
Location photographs © 2010 by Somchai Phongphaisarnkit,
  except p7, p9 (middle) © Getty Images

Design: Jane Humphrey
Photography: Will Heap and Somchai Phongphaisarnkit
Editor: Vicky Orchard
Copy editor: Penny Phillips
Americanizer: Jo Richardson
Food stylist: Annie Nicholls
Props stylist: Wei Tang
Production: Gemma John

Color reproduction by Scanhouse in Malaysia
Printed and bound in China by C & C Offset Printing Co., Ltd.

For David Sweetman

Noodles

INTRODUCTION

Although I am Thai, I have lived in London, England all my adult life. During my time there, I have become accustomed to the idea that most locals do not think of me as specifically Thai but just as being from "somewhere in the East," most probably China. I imagine that, in the same way, most Westerners eating or looking at a dish of noodles have no idea where it comes from or what it is in it. This book aims to provide some of the answers.

For many Americans and Europeans, the main significance of Asian noodles is that they supposedly inspired the invention of spaghetti. Marco Polo is said to have brought some samples back to Italy after his pioneering journey to China. But aside from being dubious historically (the Italians probably ate some forms of pasta in ancient times and acquired the habit of making it into long strands from the Arabs), this legend promotes the idea that the only worthwhile noodles are European. In fact, nothing could be farther from the truth. Asian noodles form a category of food that makes the spectrum of pasta dishes look narrow. They embrace the cuisines of several nations rather than just one and are often made from grains and beans besides wheat. As a result, they offer an unrivaled diversity of eating experiences.

烧米粉 6元

丸米粉 6元

丸米粉 6元

丸米粉 6元

肉丝米粉 6元

辣笋粉 6元

烧猪肚粉 7元

爆大肠粉 6元

干半米粉 6元

米粉 5元

A Westerner arriving in Asia for the first time may be surprised to discover roadside stalls selling noodles in almost every village, town, and city center. The noodles on offer come in many different varieties. Some are made from wheat flour, others from rice, mung beans, and other sources of starch. The noodles can be thin or thick, long or short; and they come in a number of different colors. Each type has a slightly different taste and texture.

Freshly cooked in a soup or a stir-fry, noodles are served with a choice of ingredients—vegetables, meats, fish, or seafood, or any combination of these—and with condiments including fish sauce, chili oil, sugar, and vinegar. They are eaten for breakfast, lunch, dinner, or as a late-night snack, and are Asia's oldest and most popular fast food.

In this book I hope to help you learn about the different types of noodle, a little of their history, how to cook noodles easily at home, and how to achieve the textures and tastes you enjoy.

HISTORY OF THE NOODLE

The earliest-known noodles were discovered in Qinghai in the northwest of China in 2005. They were found inside a sealed bowl buried beneath several yards of sediment. Made from a combination of broomcorn and foxtail millet, the long, thin yellow noodles have been dated to around 2000 BCE.

Noodle-making grew in popularity following the development of large scale wheat-grinding technology during the second half of the Han dynasty (206 BCE–220 CE). The oldest written reference to noodles appears in a poem written by the Chinese scholar Shu Hsi around 300 CE. He describes them as being "mainly the invention of the common people, though some of the cooking methods come from foreign lands."

Once noodles were well established in China, it was only a matter of time before the habit of eating them spread to other parts of Asia. A millennium and a half ago, China was the most populous and advanced nation in the world, with strong trading links with many of its neighbors. By 1000 CE, there were Chinese communities in the areas that later became Korea, Siam, Burma, Vietnam, Japan, the Philippines, Malaysia, and Indonesia. Over the following centuries, many Chinese people displaced by war, famine, or economic hardship migrated to these communities, bringing their cooking methods and traditions with them. As time went by, they modified their favorite recipes to suit local ingredients, creating a range of early fusion foods in which noodles played a major part.

Many of the recipes in this book are local variations of the same basic noodle dishes, adapted over time and each with its own individual tastes and name. The characteristic flavors vary considerably from country to country, but the Chinese origin is betrayed by the local names for noodles. Known as *mian* or *mien* or *mi* in their country of origin, they became *men* in Japan, *myun* in Korea, and *mee* in Thailand.

Originally noodles were always made and cooked fresh, but it was soon discovered that they could be sun-dried for storage and transport. The dried noodles then needed only a few minutes' immersion in hot water to be ready for cooking. Noodles are now manufactured widely, from small stores making them by the ancient technique of hand-pulling to factories turning out the ubiquitous pot noodles, and are sold everywhere from the original roadside stalls to trendy noodle bars around the world.

If you visit a noodle bar, you will see different meats, vegetables, noodles, and stock on display, and you and the chef decide what particular combination to cook. Likewise with the recipes in this book, if you want to change the suggested type of noodle or meat, feel free to experiment.

THE JOY OF NOODLES

For me and billions of other Asians, eating noodles is second nature. We have been doing it since we were infants and for us their merits are obvious. Nevertheless, we recognize that those who have not grown up in this way may need a little persuasion to throw themselves into the wonderful world of noodles. Here, then, is a list of some of their chief virtues:

Versatility—Asian noodles can be prepared in an almost infinite number of ways. Whether you want dinner or a nourishing breakfast, a substantial meal or a snack, a wet dish or a dry one, something spicy or something comforting, there are thousands of noodle-based recipes that fit the bill.

Convenience—Most noodles need very little cooking time, so preparing them is quick and easy. This is a big advantage in today's time-pushed world. They are also often available in dried form, which gives them long shelf lives and makes them easy to store.

Availability—As well as specialist internet sites, there are Asian food markets and grocery stores all over the world, so obtaining even fairly obscure kinds of noodle should not prove too difficult. All those Chinese and Thai restaurants must be getting their supplies from somewhere!

Healthfulness—Making noodles is an excellent way of capturing the nutrients present in grains and beans. Noodles are good, easily digestible sources of energy-yielding carbohydrates and are usually completely free of artificial preservatives. They are also typically cooked with fresh ingredients, which makes eating them an even healthier option.

Mouthfeel—A description of the advantages of eating noodles that left out how they feel in the mouth would be ignoring one of their main attractions. Noodles are quite simply fun to eat—just watch a child consuming a bowlful of them. They stimulate the lips, tongue, and appetite, particularly in countries where slurping is encouraged.

Texture—The cuisines of the East have always been more interested in texture than their Western equivalents. Noodles provide plenty of options in this department. They can be anything from soft and chewy to crisp and crunchy—the result all depends on how they are prepared.

Flavor Retention—Noodles are superb holders of the tastes of the dishes in which they appear. They easily become coated with sauces and readily absorb the flavors of stocks.

International Diversity—Eating noodles is an enjoyable and unthreatening way to explore the cuisines of many different countries. A delicate Japanese soup is a world away from a fiery Thai salad, but both can be made with exactly the same noodles.

NOODLES

The basic ingredients of noodles are flour or starch and water, mixed together to form a dough, which is then either rolled into sheets and cut into strands or extruded by machine. In some parts of Asia, noodles are still formed by hand: the dough is rolled on a table, then stretched by hand into thinner and thinner strands. The main types of noodle are covered in this book, but there are many others. They can be made from all sorts of constituents, including soybeans, potato, sweet potato, seaweed, agar agar, and cornstarch.

Most machine-made noodles are dried and packaged; freshly-made ones are usually cooked immediately, although they can be kept in the refrigerator for a few days.

In many of the smaller noodle-making stores in Asia, the noodles are cut, then put on large sheets and left to dry in the sun. Originally this was the only way to dry them, because the small stores could not afford drying ovens. Now, of course, sun-dried produce has become fashionable again.

In Bangkok, there used to be a number of restaurants where noodles were freshly made on the premises. The father would make them, the mother cook them, and the children serve them—a real family business. As a youngster I loved to visit these restaurants and see the dough being rolled out, thrown around in the air to create the noodles, and then transformed into food on my plate. Going to these places was excellent entertainment even if you weren't eating. Nowadays you can experience something similar at some of the bigger hotel restaurants, when specialist chefs are brought in to demonstrate the art of making noodles by hand.

Recently, in a street food market in Beijing, I came across a stall with a large bowl containing a mound of noodle dough. Seemingly at the speed of light, the vendor whirred a grater around the dough mound, forming a single long, thin noodle. Although this looked and may sound simple, it took a lot of practice to do it without the noodle falling to pieces. Peeling an apple in one strand is easy by comparison!

COOKING

Dried noodles are usually briefly cooked (blanched) in boiling water, the immersion time varying according to the type of noodle. They are then drained, rinsed under cold water to stop the cooking process to prevent them from becoming sticky, then drained again. Having been blanched, the noodles can be stir-fried

or deep-fried if a recipe calls for it. Fresh noodles will generally need to be separated on removal from the package, but they can then be stir-fried or deep-fried without needing to be blanched.

As a general rule, the cooking directions you find on packages of noodles are accurate and can be followed with confidence. The only problem you may occasionally encounter is the directions being printed solely in an unfamiliar Asian language!

COOKING UTENSILS

For blanching I suggest using an ordinary pan and a wooden-handled strainer, or a small wire-mesh basket—again with a wooden handle—to hold the noodles in the water while they are being cooked. They can then easily be removed from the boiling water, rinsed in a pan of cold water, and left to drain, staying in the same strainer or wire-mesh basket throughout the process.

For frying, although you can use a large pan, it is best to use a wok. Woks are versatile—they can be used for boiling or soaking as well as for frying—and when used for stir-frying they require a minimum amount of oil. After use, the wok should be scrubbed in hot water with a brush without detergent. Dry the wok by hand and place it over low heat for a minute to evaporate any residual moisture. This should prevent rusting.

NOODLES AND TRADITION

Noodles are such a big part of daily life in Asia that they have inevitably acquired all sorts of cultural significance. In China, they are generally served uncut because, according to tradition, they represent long life. Only someone very unsuperstitious would dream of risking shortening their lifespan by chopping them into smaller pieces.

In many parts of Asia, noodles are a compulsory part of meals to celebrate occasions such as birthdays and weddings. They are also closely associated with New Year. In Japanese households, it is traditional to see out the old year with a bowl of soba noodles. Another local custom is for people to make gifts of the same noodles to their neighbors when they move into an area. The origin of this practice probably lies in the fact that the word *soba* means "next to" as well as "buckwheat noodles."

A fine noodle-related Asian tradition worth mentioning is their role as a kind of bridge between the living and the dead. Bereaved relatives and friends often bring bowls of noodles as graveside offerings to the deceased, especially on the twenty-fourth day of the lunar month.

REGIONAL SPECIALTIES

China—Historically, the noodles consumed in a particular area reflected the crops that were easiest to grow there. People in the north of China typically ate wheat-based noodles, while southerners made theirs from rice flour. Today, both kinds of noodle are readily available throughout the country. Wheat-based noodles are known as *mien* (or *mein*), as in *chow mein*, China's most famous noodle dish. They can be made with or without eggs and are often sprinkled with cornstarch to prevent them sticking together. Yellowish egg noodles are particularly popular in the south. Rice noodles are known as *fen* or *fan* in China. The most commonly eaten ones, which are thin and opaque, puff up when cooked in hot oil.

Japan—The Japanese eat more noodles than any other people. The national obsession with them is celebrated in the movie *Tampopo*, which is well worth watching if you get the chance. The three most important varieties of noodle in Japan are *udon*, which are thick, round, and made from wheat flour; Chinese-style wheat noodles known as *ramen*, and *soba*, which are thin, grayish-brown, slightly

nutty in flavor, and made with a combination of buckwheat and regular flour. One popular variation of *soba* contains powdered green tea.

Korea—The culture of noodles in the Korean peninsula is similar to Japan's, reflecting the countries' geographical proximity. One distinctive variety is called *tang meon*. Made with sweet potato and cornstarch, it has a rubbery texture similar to that of the mung bean noodles popular in other parts of Asia.

Thailand—We Thais use several types of noodle in our cooking, ranging from the ribbonlike rice noodles at the heart of *pad thai* to slippery mung bean threads known as *woon sen*. One type of dish that is more popular in Thailand than elsewhere is the noodle salad.

Vietnam—Mung bean noodles play an important part in Vietnamese cuisine, particularly thin, glassy ones, which are used in soups and as fillings for spring rolls. Rice noodles are also very popular, as they are derived from the region's dominant crop. *Malaysia and Singapore*—The definitive noodle dish in Malaysia is a spicy soup or stew known as *laksa*. Singapore fried noodles, meanwhile, are justifiably famous and they appear on Chinese restaurant menus all over the world.

Other countries—Noodles feature prominently in the cooking of several other Asian nations. In Cambodia and Laos, the noodle culture resembles that of Vietnam. Burmese noodle dishes often have currylike flavors, while those of the Philippines are sometimes influenced by Spanish cuisine.

ORDERING NOODLES

Asian noodles sold at street stalls are still thought of as "fast food." Whoever takes your order will ask what type of noodle you want—big, small, egg, and so on—and whether you want them cooked as a soup, "dry," or stir-fried. Your order will be served within minutes.

I eat noodles every day, whether for breakfast, lunch, dinner, or late supper, yet I always order the same combinations: egg noodles with roast duck, vermicelli noodle soup with beef, Thai fried noodles with shrimp; many different dishes, but always the same

combinations. Like most people, when I was young I found out which ones I like best.

EATING NOODLES

There are many different eating habits across Southeast Asia. In China and Japan, noodles are eaten with the bowl held close to the mouth; you transfer the noodles from bowl to mouth using chopsticks, making slurping noises as you do so. The slurping noises are part of social etiquette and signify your enjoyment of the noodles; eating slowly and quietly is considered strange. Slurping also helps to cool hot noodles and the oxygen taken in is said to enhance their flavor. In Korea and Taiwan, however, noisy eating is not appreciated and the bowl is left on the table.

In some countries it is polite to offer food from your own chopsticks to a friend or relative; in other countries this is frowned upon. As always, if you are in a situation where you are unsure of the table etiquette, watch what the other diners are doing!

When are noodles eaten?
There are noodle dishes that can be eaten for breakfast, a mid-morning snack, lunch, an afternoon snack, dinner, or late supper—in short, anytime. Having noodles for breakfast may sound strange, but when you think about it, it isn't so different from the Western habit of eating cereals at the beginning of the day. In Asia, you will find some noodle stalls that serve only from early morning to afternoon, while others serve from late afternoon until the following morning.

CHOPSTICKS

Chopsticks are used in most Asian countries for eating noodle dishes. In Thailand, chopsticks are used only for eating noodles, while a fork and spoon are used for eating rice dishes.

The length of chopsticks differs between countries, as does the shape. In China, for example, they are square at the end you hold and round at the other end, whereas in Japan things are often the other way round. Most countries also have much longer chopsticks — up to 12 inches or 16 inches—that are used in the kitchen for cooking only.

Traditionally, chopsticks were made mainly from bamboo or wood, with silver and jade being used for special occasions. For some time silver chopsticks were believed to detect poison in food. In fact, all that was happening was certain types of food reacting with the metal to cause discoloration.

Nowadays chopsticks are made from a variety of materials, mainly wood. Natural wood has a mildly antibacterial property and in restaurants chopsticks are normally presented in a pack with the sticks still joined to show they have not been used. It has been estimated that 30 million trees a year are cut down just to manufacture disposable chopsticks; there are now moves to educate people to use metal or plastic ones instead.

CONDIMENTS

Noodles are always cooked and served with the assumption that the final taste is to be determined by the person eating them, using the condiments that are invariably served alongside. You adjust the cooked dish to suit your own preferred taste. In Asia, the four flavors used are salt, sour, spice, and sweet.

Saltiness is given by fish sauce, a pungent, strongly flavored condiment made from fish left to ferment in barrels for months. It ranges in color from light to dark brown. Fish sauce is high in vitamins and protein, making it a useful dietary asset.

Saltiness can also come from soy sauce, which is made from soybeans mixed with roasted grain and similarly left to ferment for months. Soy sauce has been in use in China and Japan for thousands of years. There are two main varieties: dark soy sauce, which is thicker, fuller-bodied, and slightly less salty;

and light soy sauce, which is thinner, saltier, and more often used as a table condiment. Nowadays there are many modifications, some with added ingredients peculiar to China and Japan as well as Indonesia and Malaysia. Each imparts an individual taste.

Sourness is provided by lime, which may be served in wedges or as a juice, or by white vinegar. Sometimes these liquids are served with small chiles soaked in them.

Spiciness is given by fresh small red or green chiles, which can be freshly chopped, broiled, or sun-dried. Red chili powder, chili oil, chili sauce, and ground white or black pepper can also be used.

Sweetness is given with white or brown sugar.

Different countries have additional regional variations: pickled garlic, pickled vegetables, and pickled shallots as well as fresh garlic and shallots are often on the table. Crushed roasted peanuts and dry-fried sesame seeds may also be served.

TYPES OF NOODLE

Asian noodles are made from a variety of flour pastes: wheat, rice, mung bean, buckwheat, seaweed, corn, and even devil's tongue, a plant related to the arum lily. The flour and water are mixed into dough, left to settle, and then cut into strips. These can be as short or long and thick or thin as the maker desires. Some noodles are plain, others are enriched with egg. Dried wheat noodles, with or without egg, are often called longevity noodles because of their association with long life.

Wheat noodles are made from plain wheat flour and water. They come in all shapes and sizes, round or flat, thick or thin, and are available, fresh, precooked, or dried.

Egg noodles are made with flour, water, and eggs. Usually wheat-flour- or rice-based, they are probably the most common type of noodle in Asia. Egg noodles are sold in various sizes and can be either dried or fresh. Fresh ones can be refrigerated for up to a week.

"Cellophane," "transparent," or "glass" noodles are made from mung bean flour (the same plant is used to produce bean sprouts). The fine, brittle strands are firm and remain so when cooked. Available only in dried form, they are almost tasteless but have a great texture and absorb the tastes of other ingredients very well. These noodles are now made in a variety of different flavors and colors—pumpkin gives a yellow tinge, seaweed a black or brown tinge, and so on.

Buckwheat noodles are usually sold dried in bundles of fine strands. Used mainly in Korea and Japan, they are also sometimes made with powdered green tea mixed into the dough. In Japan, buckwheat noodles are known as *soba*.

Rice vermicelli is, or are, one of the most popular and versatile kinds of noodle.

("Vermicelli" is the Italian for "little worms," hence the grammatical ambiguity). Unlike most noodles, which are made from a mixture of ingredients, rice noodles are made from just one: whole grains of rice, soaked in water and ground into a paste, which is then strained to form a dough. Vermicelli come in various shapes and sizes, and are sold in both fresh and sun-dried forms.

Dried rice noodle sticks are broader and thicker than vermicelli, and can be timed to retain their al dente texture during cooking.

COOKING METHODS

Fresh noodles can be cooked directly, whereas dried ones need to be soaked in water for a short while and rinsed before cooking. Follow the package directions. As indicated earlier, noodles are often cooked twice: first they are blanched, then they are fried.

Noodle soups—The noodles are blanched in boiling water, then cooked with meat, fish, and/or vegetables and served in a tasty broth.

Dried noodles—Again the noodles are blanched in boiling water and cooked with the other ingredients, but this time they are mixed with a sauce before serving.

Deep-fried noodles—The noodles are deep-fried, then they are either mixed with a sauce or a sauce is poured on top.

Stir-fried noodles—The noodles are stir-fried in a wok with meat and vegetables.

Fuzhou
Flour
Vermicelli

INGREDIENTS: Flour
NET WT : 300g
Made in China

Stock recipes

MEAT STOCK

about 1½ pounds meat bones or poultry carcasses

Remember, if you keep the stock you must boil it every day, or pour it into containers and freeze it.

1 In a large pan, cover the bones or carcasses with 1½ quarts water, bring to a boil, and simmer for 2 hours, skimming any foam off the surface from time to time, and adding water as necessary to cover the bones. Add no herbs or spices; these will be added according to each individual recipe. Strain the liquid.

Dashi

JAPANESE STOCK

1 sheet (approx. 6 inches x 8 inches) dried seaweed (*kombu*)
3 tablespoons shredded dried bonito flakes (*katsuobushi*)

1 In a large pan, bring 1½ quarts water to a boil. Rinse the seaweed under cold water and add to the boiling water, stirring continuously for 3 minutes.
2 Remove the seaweed from the water, then add the shredded bonito. Bring back to a boil, stirring continuously, then remove the pan from the heat and let stand for 5 minutes. Strain the liquid.

VEGETABLE STOCK

1 medium onion, peeled and halved
2 medium carrots, coarsely chopped
2 celery stalks, coarsley chopped
4 cilantro stems
1 teaspoon whole black peppercorns

Other vegetables may be substituted if desired, but avoid highly flavored or colored ones, such as beets. Do not add any other herbs or spices.

1 In a large pan, cover all the ingredients with 1½ quarts water, bring to a boil, and simmer for 1 hour. Strain the liquid.

CHICKEN AND DUCK

Noodles

My visits to Singapore always give me impressions of cleanliness, order, and a tremendous ethnic mix. It was also here that I had my first experience of multicultural foods.

Fusion food, which is generally seen as a marriage of Western and Eastern cuisines, has become very fashionable during the last decade. If you look at the history of cooking, however, it is apparent that the process has been going on for hundreds of years. One of the most colorful and well-known examples of fusion cuisine is the Nonya food of Malaysia and Singapore. By the fifteenth century, many Chinese people had migrated to large trading bases established in Penang and Malacca. Malay-born Chinese did not often intermarry with the local Muslim population, preferring to marry women from China instead. The resulting families, known as Nonya, partly assimilated themselves into the Malay culture, particularly when it came to food, dress, and language, but they also retained aspects of their Chinese heritage, such as their names and religion. The bonds within these families were very strong, as can be seen today in the "clan" houses of Penang, where the family trees of the members of that particular clan are displayed, stretching all the way back to the original emigrants from China.

Nonya cuisine retains many of the basics brought from China, particularly noodles, but they have been mixed with local ingredients such as belacan (shrimp paste), galangal, lemongrass, and chiles to create a unique cooking style. The most famous Nonya dishes are *laksa* (curried noodles) and Singapore noodles (stir-fried noodles with curry powder). The amalgamation of Chinese and Malay cultures is not limited to the kitchen; the Nonya gradually adapted many of their traditions and festivals as they took in Malay influences.

Tom Ka Wunsen

DUCK, VERMICELLI, AND COCONUT SOUP

Coconut milk is made from the flesh of the coconut. It is soaked in warm water, then squeezed to make the milk. It is available fresh, in cartons, in cans, or as a powder.
Serves 4

I quart chicken stock
2-inch piece galangal, peeled and
  cut lengthwise into thin sticks
¼ cup fish sauce
4 kaffir lime leaves, chopped
½ pound duck breast fillet,
  finely sliced
8 small red chiles, crushed

1 cup coconut milk
4 ounces mung bean vermicelli
  noodles, cooked according to
  the package directions and
  drained
¼ cup fresh lime juice
cilantro leaves, to garnish

1 In a saucepan, heat the stock, add the galangal, fish sauce, and kaffir lime leaves, and then bring to a boil, stirring continuously.
2 Add the duck, chiles, and coconut milk, and continue to cook, stirring, until the duck is cooked through. Then add the noodles and lime juice, stir for a few seconds, and pour into 4 serving bowls. Garnish with cilantro leaves and serve.

THAILAND Ba Mee Ped Yang

EGG NOODLES WITH ROAST DUCK

Annatto seed, also called achiote, comes from a small flowering tree and is small, red-brown, and almost triangular. The seed is usually fried in oil or fat until it releases its color and fragrance; then it is discarded and the oil is used in various recipes. Annatto seed is often used by the Chinese to color foods.
Serves 4 to 6

For the roast duck
1 duck, weighing about 4½ pounds
1 tablespoon annatto (achiote) seed
2 tablespoons sweet soy sauce
1 tablespoon five-spice powder
1 tablespoon sugar
4 garlic cloves, finely chopped
1 tablespoon ground white pepper
½ tablespoon salt

For the noodles
4 to 6 bunches egg noodles,
  cooked according to the package
  directions, drained, and tossed
  with garlic oil
4 scallions, finely chopped,
  to garnish

1 Pour boiling water over the duck, then drain it well.
2 To make the marinade, first crush the annatto (achiote) seed and cook in ½ cup boiling water for 15 minutes. Strain and mix with the soy sauce, five-spice powder, sugar, garlic, pepper, and salt.
3 Place the duck on a rack over a roasting pan. Pour some of the marinade into the cavity of the duck, then close with a skewer. Brush half the remaining marinade over the skin. Roast in a preheated oven at 350°F for 45 minutes.
4 Remove from the oven and brush again with the remaining marinade. Roast for another 45 minutes at 300°F. Remove from the oven and let rest for 5 minutes before carving.
5 Divide the cooked noodles among 4 to 6 serving bowls, then place the duck slices on top of the noodles, garnish with the scallions, and serve.

Shijin Chaomein

FRIED NOODLES WITH DUCK AND SHRIMP

Bamboo grows all over Asia. The young shoots have a unique sappy flavor and a crunchy texture. Fresh shoots always need boiling first; those in a can are ready-cooked.

Serves 4

6 ounces duck, boned and shredded

1 tablespoon soy sauce

1 teaspoon sugar

2 teaspoons cornstarch

¾ pound egg noodles

2 eggs

salt

3 tablespoons vegetable oil

4 scallions, cut into 1-inch lengths

¾ cup canned, drained or cooked fresh sliced bamboo shoots, shredded

3½ cups fresh spinach leaves (or other green vegetable), shredded

3½ ounces raw medium shrimp, peeled and deveined

2 tablespoons chicken stock or water

1 Put the duck in a bowl with the soy sauce, sugar, and cornstarch, and mix well. Cover and let marinate for 20 minutes.

2 Cook the noodles according to the package directions, drain, and rinse under cold water, then drain again and set aside.

3 Beat the eggs with a little salt. Heat 1 tablespoon of the vegetable oil in a skillet over low heat, add the beaten egg, and cook to make a thin omelet. Remove from the pan and cut into ½-inch strips.

4 Heat another 1 tablespoon of the oil in the pan, add the duck, and stir-fry until the duck starts to change color, then remove from the pan and set aside.

5 Heat the remaining 1 tablespoon oil in the pan, add the scallions, then the bamboo shoots, spinach, and a little salt, and stir-fry briefly. Add the shrimp and return the duck and the egg strips.

6 Mix the ingredients thoroughly, adding the stock or water to moisten. Stir in the noodles, heat through, and stir-fry until until there is no liquid left in the pan and the shrimp have completely changed color. Serve.

Bamboo grows all over Asia. The young shoots have a unique sappy flavor and a crunchy texture.

FIVE-SPICE DUCK WITH NOODLE SOUP

Five-spice powder is an aromatic Chinese concoction with a unique flavor that makes it a valuable seasoning and a condiment. It is made from an ancient formula, using three spices native to the area—star anise, cassia bark, and Sichuan peppercorns—together with the seed of wild fennel and clover from the nearby Molucca islands.

Serves 6

8 garlic cloves, crushed

4 cilantro roots, washed and crushed

1-inch piece galangal, peeled and thinly sliced

15 black peppercorns, crushed

1 cinnamon stick

5 star anise

3 tablespoons five-spice powder

1 tablespoon salt

2 tablespoons sugar

3 tablespoons light soy sauce

2 tablespoons dark soy sauce

1 duck, weighing about 4 pounds

For the noodles

10 ounces rice stick noodles, soaked in warm water for 5 minutes, rinsed under cold water, and drained

1 cup fresh bean sprouts

4 scallions, finely chopped

1 Place 2½ quarts water and all the ingredients, except the duck and those for the noodles, in a large pan and bring to a boil. Add the duck, bring back to a boil, and simmer for 45 to 60 minutes.

2 Remove the duck from the liquid, let the duck and the broth cool, then remove the meat from the bones and set aside. Reheat the broth.

3 Dip the noodles in boiling water for a few seconds, then divide the noodles among 6 serving bowls. Place the bean sprouts and duck meat on top of the noodles, then pour the warm broth over. Garnish with the scallions and serve.

Five-spice is made from an ancient formula, using three spices native to the area—star anise, cassia bark, and Sichuan peppercorns—together with the seed of wild fennel and clover from the nearby Molucca islands.

Vit Xao Mang

DUCK NOODLE SOUP

Any celebration meal in Southeast Asia will include a noodle dish, as noodles are associated with long life. This dish will be served in most Vietnamese homes on New Year's Eve.
Serves 8

5 shallots, crushed
1 duck, weighing 3½ to 4½ pounds
1 tablespoon salt
1 teaspoon freshly ground black pepper
½ cup canned, drained sliced bamboo shoots, shredded
1 teaspoon sugar
3 tablespoons fish sauce
8 ounces medium rice noodles

To garnish
1 tablespoon chopped scallion
1 tablespoon chopped cilantro leaves

1 Rub the crushed shallots over the duck, then sprinkle the salt and pepper all over it, cover, and let stand in the refrigerator for 1 hour.
2 In a large pan, bring 5 cups water to a boil. Add the duck and bamboo shoots, bring back to a boil, and simmer for 15 minutes. Add the sugar, then cover and simmer for 1 hour. Add the fish sauce, cover again, and simmer until the duck has a chewy texture, another 30 minutes.
3 Meanwhile, cook the noodles in 2 quarts boiling water for 5 minutes, or according to the package directions. Drain and rinse under cold water, then drain again.
4 Serve the noodles in 8 serving bowls. Remove the duck from the soup and cut it into 8 pieces. Place one piece and some bamboo shoots into each bowl, then cover with the soup. Garnish with the scallion and cilantro, and serve.

SHANGHAI EGG NOODLES WITH DEEP-FRIED DUCK

The duck in this dish is traditionally chopped and cooked with the bone, as this gives extra flavor, but if you wish you can use duck fillets instead.
Serves 4

4 tablespoons Chinese rice wine
4 tablespoons light soy sauce
4 tablespoons dark soy sauce
2 tablespoons sugar
1 tablespoon pounded fresh ginger
2 large garlic cloves, crushed
½ teaspoon five-spice powder
1 duck, weighing about 4½ pounds, chopped into 12 pieces
about 1 cup vegetable oil, for deep-frying
3 tablespoons fresh lime juice
4 to 6 bunches egg noodles, cooked according to the package directions, drained, and tossed in 2 tablespoons sesame oil

To garnish
cilantro sprigs
lime wedges

1 In a bowl, mix 2 tablespoons of the rice wine, 2 tablespoons of the light soy sauce, 2 tablespoons of the dark soy sauce, and all the sugar. Stir the mixture until the sugar has dissolved, then add the ginger, garlic, and five-spice powder, and stir well. Rub the mixture into the duck pieces, then place them on the perforated section of a heated steamer. Cover and steam for 20 minutes. Let the duck cool and then dry thoroughly with paper towels.
2 Heat the oil in a wok and fry the duck pieces until they are golden brown all over. Remove using a skimmer and drain over the pan.
3 Reheat the oil in the wok, add the remainder of the rice wine and soy sauces, and stir well. Add the lime juice and simmer briefly, then place the duck in the sauce and stir before transferring to a serving dish.
4 Serve the noodles with the duck, garnished with cilantro sprigs and lime wedges.

The duck is traditionally chopped and cooked with the bone, as this gives extra flavor, but if you wish you can use duck fillets.

Mian Bao Ya

DUCK AND NOODLES WITH MUSHROOMS AND BELL PEPPERS

Chinese rice wine is made from fermented glutinous rice; the best is reputed to come from Shaoxing in Northeast China. If rice wine is unavailable, a dry sherry can be used.

Serves 4

For the sauce

1 pound skinless duck fillets, finely ground

2 cups duck or chicken stock

¾ cup (¾ ounce) dried wood ear (cloud ear) mushrooms, soaked in warm water for 20 minutes, drained, stems discarded, and thinly sliced

2 medium onions, finely chopped

1 red bell pepper, seeded, and cut into thin strips

3 tablespoons Chinese rice wine

2 tablespoons light soy sauce

2 tablespoons dark soy sauce

1 tablespoon rice flour or cornstarch

1 tablespoon sesame oil

½ teaspoon salt

For the noodles

¼ cup vegetable oil

10 ounces flat rice stick noodles, soaked in warm water for 10 minutes, rinsed under cold water, and drained

1 tablespoon dark soy sauce

1 Place the duck and the stock in a pan and bring to a boil. Skim off any fat from the surface, then add the mushrooms, onions, and bell pepper. Pour in the rice wine and soy sauces, stir well, and simmer for 4 minutes.

2 Mix the rice flour or cornstarch with 3 tablespoons cold water and stir into the contents of the pan. Cook, stirring continuously, until the mixture thickens slightly, then simmer for another 2 minutes.

3 To make the noodles, in a wok, heat the vegetable oil and fry the noodles for 2 minutes, then add the soy sauce. Mix well, then divide the noodles among 4 serving plates.

4 Immediately before serving, stir the sesame oil and salt into the duck sauce, then pour it over the noodles.

If rice wine is unavailable, a dry sherry can be used.

FRIED NOODLES WITH CHICKEN AND VEGETABLES

Bok choy is characterized by fleshy stems and green flat leaves with a mustard taste. The leaves and the stems are used in soups and stir-fries or as vegetables in salads.

Serves 4

6 tablespoons peanut oil

1 large onion, sliced

1 pound skinless chicken breast fillets, cut into thin strips

4 chicken livers, cut into small cubes

2 tablespoons light soy sauce

½ pound bok choy, shredded

2 celery stalks, thinly sliced

5 scallions, cut into 2-inch lengths

4 dried Chinese black (shiitake) mushrooms, soaked in warm water for 30 minutes, drained, stems discarded, and thinly sliced

3 eggs

salt and pepper

½ pound Chinese egg noodles, cooked according to the package directions, rinsed under cold water, and drained

1 Heat 4 tablespoons of the peanut oil in a wok and stir-fry the onion until golden. Add the chicken strips, then the chicken livers and cook until the chicken changes color. Stir in the soy sauce, then all the vegetables and mushrooms, and gently stir-fry for 3 minutes. Place in a warmed dish and set aside.

2 Lightly beat the eggs with 2 tablespoons water, and season with salt and pepper. Heat another 1 tablespoon of the oil in the wok, add the eggs, and stir-fry until scrambled, then transfer to a plate and set aside.

3 Heat the remaining 1 tablespoon oil in the wok and stir-fry the noodles for 3 to 4 minutes. Remove from the pan and spread onto a warmed shallow dish. Spoon over the meat and vegetable mixture, top with the scrambled egg, and serve.

RICE STICK NOODLES WITH CHICKEN AND DRIED SHRIMP

The dried shrimp, which would originally have been sun-dried, gives the recipe a salty, fishy flavor.
Serves 4

¼ cup vegetable oil

½ pound skinless chicken breast fillets, cut into ½-inch cubes

½ cup canned, drained sliced bamboo shoots, cut into thin sticks

2 tablespoons dried shrimp, soaked in warm water for
    10 minutes, drained, and finely chopped

1 leek, cut into thin sticks

1 celery stalk, cut into thin sticks

1 teaspoon salt

¼ cup chicken stock

1 pound rice stick noodles, soaked in warm water for 5 minutes, rinsed
    under cold water, and drained

4 small dried Chinese black (shiitake) mushrooms, soaked in warm water
    for 30 minutes, drained, stems discarded, and cut into 1-inch strips

2 tablespoons soy sauce

1 Heat 2 tablespoons of the vegetable oil in a wok, add the chicken, bamboo shoots, shrimp, leek, celery, salt, and stock, and stir-fry for 2 minutes. Remove and set aside.

2 Heat the remainder of the oil in the wok and stir-fry the noodles for 2 to 3 minutes, then add the chicken mixture, mushrooms, and soy sauce. Cook until there is no juice left, about another 2 minutes, then serve.

The dried shrimp, which would originally have been sun-dried, gives the recipe a salty, fishy flavor.

CHICKEN SPRING ROLLS

These are the classic, deep-fried Vietnamese spring rolls. They are one of the most popular dishes in Vietnam.

Makes about 20

For the filling

1¾ ounces transparent noodles, soaked in warm water for 10 minutes, drained, and cut into 1-inch pieces

1 pound chicken breast fillets, skinned and cut into thin strips

2 tablespoons dried wood ear (cloud ear) mushrooms, soaked in warm water for 20 minutes, drained, and finely chopped

3 garlic cloves, finely chopped

3 shallots, finely chopped

½ teaspoon freshly ground black pepper

½ teaspoon salt

¾ cup finely shredded white cabbage

For the wraps

2 eggs, beaten

20 dried Vietnamese rice papers

1 cup vegetable oil

To garnish

mint leaves

cilantro leaves

1 To make the filling, put all the ingredients in a bowl and mix well.

2 To make the wraps, brush the beaten egg over the entire surface of the rice papers and leave for a few seconds until soft. Place 1 teaspoon of the filling in a rectangular shape along the curved edge of the paper, roll once, then fold the sides over to enclose the filling and continue rolling. Continue the process until all the papers are used.

3 Heat the oil in a skillet, place about one third of the spring rolls in the pan, and fry until golden brown. Remove from the oil with a slotted spoon and drain on paper towels. Repeat the process until all the rolls are cooked, and serve hot or warm, garnished with mint and cilantro leaves.

CHICKEN NOODLE SOUP

This is another version of the famous Vietnamese dish pho. When I was in Ho Chi Minh City, I saw food stalls being set up outside the old shop houses in the early morning. The owners would set up cauldrons of pho soup and surround them with tables and chairs that were quickly filled by the locals.
Serves 4

For the soup
vegetable oil, for brushing
6 small red shallots, peeled
2 small onions, cut into small squares
1¾ ounces fresh ginger, peeled and cut into ½-inch squares
2 quarts chicken stock
2 tablespoons fish sauce
1 teaspoon salt
1 tablespoon sugar

For the chicken noodles
9 ounces skinless chicken breast fillets, blanched in boiling water until cooked, drained, and cut into thin slices
9 ounces fresh flat noodles, blanched in boiling water until just soft, drained, and placed in a serving bowl

To garnish
2 scallions, finely chopped
2 tablespoons chopped cilantro

1 Heat a grill pan or heavy-bottomed skillet over high heat and brush with vegetable oil. Add the shallots, onions, and ginger, and cook, turning frequently, until lightly browned.
2 In a large pan, heat the stock, add the browned shallots, onions, and ginger, and bring to a boil. Reduce the heat, add the fish sauce, salt, and sugar, and simmer for 1 hour. Strain the soup and set aside.
3 Place the chicken on top of the blanched noodles. Pour the soup over, sprinkle with the scallions and cilantro to garnish, and serve.

This is another version of the famous Vietnamese dish pho.

STIR-FRIED CHICKEN NOODLES

Yakisoba is one of the most popular noodle dishes in Japan, a derivative of chow mein—this version is inspired by the original but made with soba (buckwheat) noodles.
Serves 4

1½ pounds fresh soba noodles, steamed or cooked according
   to the package directions and drained
1 tablespoon sesame oil
2 tablespoons vegetable oil
½ pound chicken breast, skinned, boned, and cut into thin slices
1 medium onion, sliced
⅔ cup carrots, cut into thin sticks
5 Chinese (napa) cabbage leaves, coarsely chopped
3 tablespoons soy sauce
1 tablespoon sugar
1 tablespoon oyster sauce
½ sheet nori (Japanese seaweed paper), shredded

1 Rinse the noodles, place them in a bowl, and stir in the sesame oil. Set aside.
2 Heat the vegetable oil in a wok and stir-fry the sliced chicken for 3 to 4 minutes. Add the onion, carrots, and cabbage, and stir-fry for another 3 to 4 minutes, then stir in the noodles, soy sauce, sugar, and oyster sauce, and mix well. Divide the mixture among 4 serving bowls, sprinkle with the shredded nori, and serve.

NOODLES WITH CHICKEN AND MIXED VEGETABLES

This dish can be served with spicy pickled vegetables and kimchi. Kimchi is a Korean specialty made by pickling vegetables and their leaves and herbs in brine. The taste varies depending on where in Korea it is made and what the maker prefers—from hot and spicy to sweet or sour, there is an infinite variety.
Serves 4

For the marinade
2 teaspoons soy sauce
3 tablespoons rice wine or pale dry sherry
2 large garlic cloves, finely chopped
2 tablespoons toasted sesame seeds
½ teaspoon sugar
1 scallion, finely sliced

1 pound skinless chicken breast fillets, thinly sliced
1 tablespoon vegetable oil
4 dried Chinese black (shiitake) mushrooms, soaked in hot water
  for 30 minutes, drained, stems discarded, and thinly sliced
2 small carrots, cut into thin sticks
1 green or red bell pepper, seeded and cut into thin sticks
1 medium onion, cut into thin sticks
1 zucchini, cut into thin sticks
2¼ ounces transparent noodles, soaked in warm water for 30 minutes,
  rinsed under cold water, and drained
1 tablespoon toasted sesame seed, to garnish

1 Place all the marinade ingredients in a bowl and mix thoroughly, then add the chicken slices, cover, and let marinate in the refrigerator for 1 hour.
2 Heat ½ tablespoon of the vegetable oil in a wok and stir-fry the vegetables, one at a time, over high heat until they are tender but still crisp, then set aside.
3 Heat the remaining ½ tablespoon oil in the wok and stir-fry the noodles—turning them so they heat evenly—until they are tender, then turn them into a warmed serving bowl.
4 Return the vegetables to the pan, add the chicken, and stir-fry until the chicken is cooked through. Place the chicken and vegetables on top of the noodles, sprinkle with the toasted sesame seed, and serve.

JAPAN Tori-Nanban

MARINATED CHICKEN WITH NOODLES

*Japanese light soy
sauce,* shoyu, *is lighter
than the Chinese
variety, and sweeter.*
Serves 4

3 skinless chicken breast fillets, sliced diagonally into bite-size pieces
2 tablespoons Japanese light soy sauce (*shoyu*)
6 cups Japanese stock (*dashi*—see page 19)
1 leek, diagonally cut into thin slices
14 ounces soba noodles
watercress, to garnish

1   Marinate the sliced chicken in the soy sauce for 15 minutes. Heat the stock in a large
pan, add the marinated chicken and the sliced leek, and bring to a boil. Simmer until
the chicken is cooked, about 15 minutes.
2   Meanwhile, bring another pan of water to a boil, add the noodles, and cook for
5 minutes, or according to the package directions. Drain and rinse under cold running
water, then drain again. Divide among 4 serving bowls.
3   Spoon the chicken, leek, and broth over the noodles, garnish with watercress, and
serve immediately.

JAPAN Kare Udon

JAPANESE NOODLES WITH CHICKEN CURRY SAUCE

*This is a modern
Japanese recipe
combining the spicy
flavor of curry sauce
with the smooth texture
of udon noodles.*
Serves 4

For the curry sauce
1 tablespoon vegetable oil
2 skinless chicken breast fillets,
    diced into ½-inch cubes
1 medium onion, sliced
2 tablespoons all-purpose flour
2 teaspoons curry powder

1¼ cups chicken stock
2 tablespoons fruit relish
½ cup dried currants
salt and pepper
1½ pounds udon noodles
5 cups hot Japanese stock (*dashi*—
    see page 19)

1   In a skillet, heat the oil and fry the chicken until cooked through, then push it to one
side and fry the onion until lightly browned. Add the flour and curry powder, mix all the
ingredients together, and stir-fry for 2 minutes, then set aside.
2   In another pan, pour in the chicken stock, then add the relish, currants, and salt and
pepper to taste. Simmer for 10 minutes, then stir in the chicken mixture.
3   Drop the noodles into boiling water and cook for 3 minutes, or according to the
package directions, then rinse under cold running water and drain. Divide the noodles
among 4 serving bowls.
4   Pour the curry sauce over the noodles, followed by the hot stock, and serve.

CHICKEN NOODLE SOUP

This noodle soup is Chinese in origin but is very popular in Thailand. It is sold from roadside stalls, on noodle boats, and by vendors who go around on tricycles, carrying all the ingredients and cooking equipment with them.
Serves 4

½ pound flat rice stick noodles

1 quart chicken stock

3 pieces dried wood ear (cloud ear) mushroom, about 2 inches in diameter, soaked in warm water for 20 minutes, drained, and finely sliced

½ teaspoon salt

3 celery stalks, finely chopped

2 scallions, cut into thin rings

10½ ounces cooked chicken, skinned and cut into thin strips

1 Cook the noodles according to the package directions, drain, and divide among 4 serving bowls.

2 In a pan, heat the stock to a simmer, add the mushrooms and salt, and cook for 3 minutes, then pour over the noodles in the bowls. Place the celery, scallions, and chicken on top and serve.

CHINA Hunan Tse Chow Mie Fun

HUNAN CHICKEN WITH EGG NOODLES

Sesame paste is made from white sesame seed that is toasted and crushed to form a paste. If you don't want to prepare it yourself, you can buy the paste in Asian markets.
Serves 4

1 chicken, weighing about 2¼ pounds

1 teaspoon salt

2 tablespoons sesame paste

1 tablespoon Chinese rice vinegar

1 tablespoon sesame oil

1 tablespoon plum sauce

1 tablespoon black peppercorns, crushed

1 tablespoon peeled and grated fresh ginger

2 scallions, finely chopped

1 garlic clove, crushed

3 tablespoons cilantro leaves

2 cups thinly sliced fresh or canned, drained water chestnuts

2 tablespoons peanut oil

½ pound cooked egg noodles

1 medium cucumber, peeled and sliced

1 Place the chicken in a large pan, cover with cold water, and add the salt. Bring to a boil and boil for 2 minutes, then cover and simmer for 1 hour. Drain and let cool, then remove the chicken from the bones and cut the meat into pieces.

2 In a bowl, mix together the sesame paste, rice vinegar, sesame oil, plum sauce, peppercorns, ginger, scallions, garlic, and cilantro. Add the chicken and water chestnuts, and stir well.

3 Heat the oil in a wok, add the noodles, and stir well, then add the chicken and sauce mixture, and cook, stirring, until heated through. Transfer to a warmed dish, garnish with the cucumber slices, and serve.

CHICKEN WITH NOODLES AND COCONUT

*This is one of the
most famous
Burmese dishes
and not difficult to
prepare at home.
Serves 6*

1 chicken, weighing about
   3¼ pounds, chopped into
   large pieces
salt
½ teaspoon ground turmeric
⅔ cup vegetable oil
3 medium onions, chopped and
   pounded
4 garlic cloves, crushed
1-inch piece fresh ginger, peeled
   and pounded
1 teaspoon chili powder
5 tablespoons yellow split pea flour
   or besan (gram or chickpea) flour
5 tablespoons lentil flour
2 cups thick coconut milk
2½ pounds fresh egg noodles

To garnish
6 garlic cloves, sliced crosswise
3 hard-boiled eggs, shelled
   and quartered
1 medium onion, sliced
4 scallions, finely chopped
1 teaspoon chili powder
2 lemons, quartered

1 Rub the chicken pieces with ½ teaspoon salt and turmeric, place in a large pan, and cover with 3 quarts cold water. Bring to a boil, then simmer until the chicken is just cooked, about 30 minutes. Remove the chicken pieces from the pan, leaving the liquid to simmer over low heat. Remove the skin and bones from the chicken pieces, cut the meat into chunks, and place it back in the simmering liquid.

2 Meanwhile, heat 6 tablespoons of the oil in a large pan, add the onions, garlic, ginger, and chili powder, and stir-fry for 5 minutes, then remove from the heat and set aside.

3 In a bowl, mix the split pea and lentil flours with about ¾ cup water to form a paste. Stir the paste into the chicken liquid and bring to a boil. Reduce the heat, add the coconut milk, and simmer, stirring frequently, until the mixture has the consistency of thick soup, about 20 minutes. Turn off the heat, cover the pan, and set aside, keeping it warm.

4 Cook the noodles in boiling salted water for 5 minutes, or according to the package directions, then drain and keep hot.

5 Heat the remaining oil in a small skillet, add a handful of the noodles, and fry quickly until crisp, then place in an individual serving bowl. Repeat the process for each guest.

6 Fry the sliced garlic in the skillet until crisp and golden, then place in a small side dish to serve with the other garnishes.

7 Place the chicken mixture in a serving dish, and serve with the noodles and garnishes.

JAVANESE NOODLES

Sambal is a fiery condiment consisting largely of chiles that can also be used as a cooking ingredient. The ulek part of the name refers to a kind of mortar and pestle traditionally used in Indonesia, particularly on the island of Java.
Serves 4

For the sambal ulek
20 small red chiles, chopped into small pieces
2 teaspoons sea salt

3 tablespoons vegetable oil
1 onion, finely sliced
2 garlic cloves, finely chopped
¾ pound chicken breast fillet, skinned and cut into bite-size pieces
¾ cup sliced white mushrooms
1 small leek, chopped into small pieces
3 celery stalks, cut into thin sticks
2 teaspoons *sambal ulek* (see above)
¾ pound egg noodles, cooked according to the package directions and drained
2 tablespoons soy sauce
½ teaspoon sugar
2 tablespoons fresh lemon juice
2 small green or red chiles, finely chopped
cilantro, to garnish

1 To make the basic chile paste, or *sambal ulek*, place the chopped chiles and sea salt in a mortar and grind into a paste. Transfer to a small jar and seal. This can be kept in the refrigator for up to 1 month.

2 Heat the oil in a wok and fry the onion until transparent, then add the garlic and chicken and stir-fry for 2 minutes. Add the mushrooms, leek, and celery and stir-fry gently for another 3 to 4 minutes.

3 Add the 2 teaspoons *sambal ulek*, then add the noodles a few at a time, followed by the soy sauce, sugar, lemon juice, and chiles, stir-frying gently until the noodles are hot. Then transfer to a warm dish, garnish with cilantro, and serve.

CHICKEN AND NOODLE SALAD

Bean sprouts are sprouted green mung beans. They can be eaten raw or blanched in salads or soups. They can also be stir-fried and served as a vegetable dish.
Serves 2

½ pound rice vermicelli noodles, soaked in warm water for 5 minutes, rinsed under cold water, and drained
6 ounces skinless chicken breast fillet
1¼ cups fresh bean sprouts
1 cup cucumber cut into 2-inch-long thin strips

1 small onion, finely chopped
3 tablespoons fish sauce
3 tablespoons fresh lime juice
1 tablespoon mint leaves, finely chopped
2 tablespoons roasted peanuts, crushed

1 In a pan, bring some water to a boil and, using a strainer, dip the noodles in the boiling water for a few seconds, then drain well, place on a large serving platter, and set aside.

2 Bring a pan of water to a boil, add the chicken, and simmer until cooked through, then remove with a slotted spoon and let cool.

3 Shred the chicken over a bowl, retaining any juices in the bowl, add all the remaining ingredients and mix well, then transfer to the noodles and serve.

CRISPY NOODLES WITH CHICKEN AND BAMBOO SHOOTS

This is one of the classic Chinese noodle dishes.
Serves 4

2 tablespoons peanut oil
10 ounces rice vermicelli noodles, soaked in warm water for 5 minutes, rinsed under cold water, and drained

For the sauce
1 egg, lightly beaten
1 tablespoon cornstarch
2 tablespoons light soy sauce
2 tablespoons dark soy sauce

1 pound skinless chicken breast fillet, thinly sliced
2 tablespoons peanut oil
1¾ cups canned, drained sliced bamboo shoots
1 tablespoon peeled and finely grated fresh ginger
½ teaspoon five-spice powder
5 tablespoons chicken stock
salt and pepper

1 Heat the oil in a wok, add the noodles, and stir-fry until golden brown, then drain and set aside.

2 For the sauce, in a bowl, lightly beat the egg, cornstarch, and soy sauces together until smooth, then fold in the sliced chicken.

3 Heat the oil in a wok, spoon in the strips of chicken, and stir-fry until just cooked through. Add the bamboo shoots, ginger, five-spice powder, and stock, and stir well, then season with salt and pepper. Turn into a warmed serving bowl and serve with the noodles.

Kyet-Tha Khauk-Swe-Byoke

BURMESE CHICKEN CURRY NOODLES

I was visiting an old friend in Rangoon and saw this dish at a street food stall. My friend refused to let me eat it there, but took me to the local market, bought the ingredients, and then cooked the dish for me at home!

Serves 4

For the curry paste

½ teaspoon coriander seed

1 teaspoon peeled and finely chopped fresh turmeric root

1 teaspoon peeled and finely chopped fresh ginger

1 large dried red chile, finely chopped

4 small red shallots, finely chopped

3 small garlic cloves, finely chopped

½ teaspoon salt

2 tablespoons peanut oil

1 tablespoon curry paste

1 cup coconut milk

10 ounces skinless chicken breast fillet, thinly sliced

2 cups chicken stock

½ pound fresh egg noodles, cooked in boiling water for 3 minutes, rinsed under cold water, and drained

2 tablespoons fish sauce

1 teaspoon sugar

1 tablespoon fresh lemon juice

3 scallions, finely chopped, to garnish

1 First make the curry paste. In a mortar, pound the coriander seed to a powder. Add the turmeric, ginger, chile, shallots, garlic, and salt, and pound together to form a paste, then set aside.

2 Heat the oil in a wok, stir in the curry paste, and add the coconut milk. Stir well, then add the chicken and stir-fry until just cooked through.

3 Pour in the stock and bring to a boil, then add the noodles, stirring continuously, followed by the fish sauce and sugar. Remove from the heat, add the lemon juice, and stir once, then turn into a large bowl, garnish with the scallions, and serve.

RICE NOODLES IN SPICY COCONUT SAUCE

Laksa is a Nonya recipe—from the Peranakan people of Singapore and Malaysia. A well-known example of the fusion of the noodle dish from China with the coconut-based curry of Singapore, it is an exotic, rich dish.

Serves 4

For the spice paste
⅓ cup finely chopped shallots
1¼–1½-inch piece fresh turmeric root, peeled and finely chopped
2 tablespoons dried shrimp
2 lemongrass stalks, finely chopped
6 slices peeled galangal
1 tablespoon coriander seed
1 teaspoon ground dried red chiles
1 teaspoon shrimp paste

For the spicy coconut sauce
2 tablespoons vegetable oil
1 quart chicken stock
1 cup coconut milk
½ teaspoon salt
½ teaspoon sugar

To serve
1¾ pounds fresh rice noodles

To garnish
8 quail eggs, hard-boiled and shelled
7 ounces skinless chicken breast fillet, blanched and shredded
7 ounces raw medium shrimp, boiled and peeled and deveined
1 cup fresh bean sprouts, lightly blanched
2 scallions, finely shredded

1 First prepare the spice paste: place all the ingredients with ¼ cup water in a mortar and grind them together until they form a smooth paste.
2 For the sauce, heat the oil in a large pan and stir in the paste, then add the stock and bring to a boil. Add the coconut milk, salt, and sugar, and heat, stirring continuously, until the mixture is hot—but do not let it boil.
3 Blanch the noodles in boiling water until just soft, drain, and divide among 4 serving bowls. Place the garnishes on top of the noodles, then ladle the spicy coconut sauce over and serve.

FRIED NOODLES WITH CHICKEN AND CHILE LIME SAUCE

The Thai word manow *means both lime and lemon, and you can substitute one for the other in this recipe.*
Serves 4

For the sauce
juice of 2 limes
4 mixed small red and green chiles, finely chopped

2 tablespoons vegetable oil
3 garlic cloves, finely chopped
14 ounces skinless chicken fillet, thinly sliced
2 cups coarsely chopped white cabbage

4 bunches egg noodles, cooked according to the package directions, rinsed under cold water, and drained
4 tablespoons Japanese light soy sauce (*shoyu*)
salt and pepper
2 scallions, finely chopped, to garnish

1 To make the sauce, mix together the lime juice and chiles and set aside.

2 Heat the oil in a wok and stir-fry the garlic and chicken until the chicken is just cooked.

3 Add the cabbage and stir well over high heat, then add the noodles, soy sauce, and salt and pepper to taste, and mix well.

4 Finally, add the chile and lime sauce, stir well to heat through, then transfer to a warm platter, garnish with the scallions, and serve.

CHICKEN NOODLE SOUP WITH CRISPY SHALLOTS

This is one of the warming winter noodle soups that are now commonly found throughout Vietnam.
Serves 4

2 tablespoons vegetable oil
2 small red shallots, finely chopped
1½ quarts chicken stock
2 tablespoons fish sauce
2 tablespoons light soy sauce
1 teaspoon sugar
1¼ cups fresh bean sprouts

½ pound flat rice stick noodles, soaked in warm water for 10 minutes, rinsed under cold water, and drained
6 ounces skinless chicken fillet, thinly sliced
3 scallions, finely chopped

1 Heat the oil in a wok and stir-fry the shallots until golden. Set aside.

2 In a pan, heat the stock. Add the fish sauce, soy sauce, and sugar, bring to a boil, and then let simmer gently.

3 Bring a large pan of water to a boil and, using a strainer, dip the bean sprouts in the water for 10 seconds, then drain well and divide among 4 serving bowls.

4 Place the noodles in the strainer, dip them in the boiling water for 20 seconds, drain, and divide among the bowls. Place the chicken strips in the strainer, dip them in the boiling water for 20 seconds, drain, and divide among the bowls.

5 Divide the broth among the bowls, sprinkle with the scallions, add ½ tablespoon of the shallot-and-oil mix to each bowl, and serve

PORK

Some friends and I recently went on a road trip. Leaving Chiang Mai, we drove through beautiful mountains and valleys to Chiang Rai, then on to Mae Sai. This border town is a popular destination for Thais, who love to visit its street markets. The local merchants sell many products from Burma and China, including antiques, electrical goods, clothing, and textiles, all noticeably cheaper than in Thailand. We then crossed the border into Burma, passing many waterfalls and panoramic views until we reached the town of Kentung in the Shan state, where we stayed overnight in a small local hotel.

Early in the morning, I went out to the local market where they were selling freshly made noodles—dried ones are not used here. Looking at the piles of noodles for sale in the market, you could see how popular they are in Kentung. When I returned to the guest house, I was duly served pork noodle soup for breakfast.

We left Kentung that morning and drove about three hours to the town of Muang La, a large casino town that, although geographically in Burma, operates as an autonomous state of China. It even uses the Chinese yuan as the local currency. If you carry on about 190 miles north from here, you arrive in an area known as Sipsong Panna in the Chinese province of Yunnan. The region is subtropical and mountainous, high on natural beauty, and was until recently very inaccessible. The capital is Jinghong, the City of the Dawn. It is also the ancient home of the Thai people. Over the centuries, many of them migrated to the areas that now form Laos, Burma, and Assam, but mostly they established themselves in Thailand. Consequently, many Thais regard Sipsong Panna as the original homeland of the Thai people.

WONTON NOODLE SOUP

Wontons are small parcels of ground meat, usually pork or chicken, wrapped in light dough sheets, about 3¼ inches square. Either meat can be used in this classic Chinese recipe. Wonton wrappers are generally available in Asian markets.

Serves 4

For the wonton filling

3 ounces ground pork or chicken meat

1 scallion, finely chopped

1 dried Chinese black (shiitake) mushroom, soaked in warm water for 30 minutes, drained, stems discarded, and finely chopped

1 teaspoon peeled and finely chopped fresh ginger

1 teaspoon light soy sauce

½ teaspoon Chinese sweet rice wine

½ teaspoon sesame oil

salt

20 wonton wrappers

10 ounces fresh thin egg noodles

1½ quarts chicken stock

2 large Iceberg lettuce leaves, halved and blanched

3 scallions, chopped

1 In a bowl, thoroughly mix together all the wonton filling ingredients. Lay a wrapper flat, and spoon 1 teaspoon of the wonton mixture onto the center. Wet the edges of the wrapper with water, then fold the wrapper over the mixture to form a clam shape, pressing out the air at the same time as sealing the edges.

2 Repeat the procedure until you have used up all the wrappers or all the mixture.

3 Bring 2 pans of water to a boil. In one pan, cook the noodles for 3 minutes, or according to the package directions. In the other, boil the wontons for 3 to 4 minutes. Drain the noodles and divide among 4 serving bowls, then top with the wontons.

4 Heat the chicken stock. Arrange the lettuce and scallions on top of the noodles, pour the heated stock over, and serve immediately.

Wontons are small parcels of ground meat, usually pork or chicken, wrapped in a light dough sheet, about 3¼ inches square.

FRIED NOODLES WITH PORK

This is a common Southeast Asian dish. The meat and seasonings are stir-fried separately, then combined with boiled noodles and stir-fried together.
Serves 4

To garnish
1 egg, beaten and fried to make a thin omelet, cooled, and
  cut into thin strips
1 medium cucumber, peeled and sliced
5 scallions, finely sliced
2 red chiles, seeded and cut into thin sticks

For the noodles and meat
2 tablespoons vegetable oil
2/3 cup thinly sliced shallots
3 large garlic cloves, finely chopped
½ pound pork tenderloin, cut into bite-size pieces
½ pound raw medium shrimp, peeled, deveined, and cut into
  small pieces
1 teaspoon hoisin sauce
½ teaspoon sugar
1 cup fresh bean sprouts
1 pound fresh rice or wheat noodles, cooked according to the package
  directions, rinsed under cold water, and drained
½ teaspoon black pepper

1 Prepare the garnishes and set aside.
2 In a wok, heat the oil and stir-fry the shallots and garlic until soft, then add the pork and shrimp and stir-fry for 2 to 3 minutes.
3 Stir in the hoisin sauce, sugar, and ½ cup water, and boil for 1 minute. Stir in the bean sprouts and cook for 30 seconds, stirring continuously.
4 Stir in the noodles until well mixed and heated through, then serve with the garnishes and pepper.

THAI CASSEROLED CRAB AND NOODLES

In Thai wunsen means bean vermicelli or glass vermicelli, which is clear when cooked, whereas rice vermicelli is known as sen mee. The tastes are slightly different, but they can be substituted for each other. This dish would traditionally have been cooked in a clay pot—glazed inside—over an open fire.
Serves 4

For the soup stock
1¾ cups pork stock (or meat stock, see page 19)
2 tablespoons oyster sauce
2 teaspoons dark soy sauce
1 teaspoon sesame oil
½ teaspoon sugar

For the crab and noodles
2 bacon slices, cut into 1-inch pieces
20 medium crab claws, without shells
1-inch piece fresh ginger, peeled and finely chopped
2 garlic cloves, crushed
1 teaspoon white peppercorns, crushed
½ pound mung bean vermicelli noodles, soaked in warm water
    for 5 minutes, rinsed under cold water, and drained
1 tablespoon sesame oil
1 teaspoon dark soy sauce
2 tablespoons coarsely chopped cilantro leaves and stems

1 Place all the soup stock ingredients in a pan and bring to a boil, then simmer for
5 minutes. Set aside.
2 In a heavy casserole dish, lay the bacon on the bottom, then cover with the crab claws,
ginger, garlic, and peppercorns. Cover with the noodles, then add the oil, soy sauce, and
soup stock. Place on the heat, cover, and bring to a boil, then simmer for 5 minutes.
3 Mix well, sprinkle with the cilantro, and cover and cook for another 5 minutes. Remove
any excess stock and serve.

This dish would traditionally have been cooked in a clay pot—glazed inside—over an open fire.

NOODLE SOUP WITH PORK AND FISHBALLS

If you do not have time to make the fishballs, they can be bought from Asian food stores. However, it is much more satisfying to make your own.

If you would like to use pig's liver, ask your local butcher if they have any in stock.
Serves 4

For the fishballs
2 pounds white fish fillets, skinned and cut into chunks
3 tablespoons cornstarch
1 egg white
salt and ground white pepper

For the noodles, meat, and vegetables
7 ounces pork tenderloin
11½ ounces rice stick noodles
3 cups fresh bean sprouts
4 tablespoons fish sauce
2 tablespoons white sugar
¼ pound pig's liver, boiled and thinly sliced (optional)
2 quarts chicken stock
12 fishballs (see above)

To garnish
2 tablespoons garlic oil
½ teaspoon ground white pepper
1 scallion, finely sliced
cilantro leaves

1 In a mortar, pound the fish and cornstarch together until they are reduced to a paste, then work in the egg white and seasoning. Wet your hands and shape the mixture into ¾-inch balls. Bring 1 quart water to the boil and boil the fishballs for 5 minutes, then remove with a slotted spoon and set aside.
2 Cook the pork in the boiling water for 15 minutes, then drain and let cool. Cut into ½-inch wide strips, cover, and set aside.
3 Place the noodles and bean sprouts in another pan, cover with water, and bring to a boil, then simmer for 3 minutes. Drain and divide among 4 serving bowls. Add 1 tablespoon fish sauce and ½ tablespoon sugar to each bowl and mix well, then top with the pork and the pig's liver.
4 Bring the chicken stock to a boil, add the fishballs, and boil for 2 minutes. Remove from the heat, divide the fishballs among the serving bowls, and fill the bowls with the stock.
5 Garnish with the garlic oil, white pepper, scallion, and cilantro leaves, and serve.

ROAST PORK LO MIEN

Five-spice powder is extremely important in Chinese cooking and is responsible for much of the flavor in this classic dish.
Serves 4

For the meat

1 pound pork tenderloin

5 garlic cloves, crushed

½ teaspoon five-spice powder

½ teaspoon salt

1 teaspoon peeled and grated fresh ginger

2 teaspoons dark soy sauce

2 tablespoons honey

2 tablespoons Chinese rice wine

For the noodles

3 tablespoons vegetable oil

1¼-inch piece fresh ginger, peeled and finely chopped

2 garlic cloves, crushed

2 small red and green bell peppers, seeded and diced

2 tablespoons black bean sauce

10 ounces flat rice stick noodles, cooked according to the package
   directions, rinsed under cold water, and drained

2 tablespoons light soy sauce

1 teaspoon sugar

1 In a large bowl, mix all the ingredients for the meat together, cover, and let marinate in the refrigerator for 2 hours.

2 Preheat the oven to 350°F. Lightly oil an oven rack, remove the meat from the marinade, and lay it on the rack in the center of the oven. Roast for 20 minutes, then brush the meat with any remaining marinade, turn, and roast for another 20 minutes. Remove from the oven and let cool, then cut into ½-inch strips.

3 Heat the remaining oil in a wok and stir-fry the ginger and garlic for 2 minutes. Add the pork, bell peppers, and black bean sauce, and stir-fry for another 2 minutes. Add the noodles, light soy sauce, and sugar, and stir-fry until the noodles are well coated with the sauce. Divide the mixture among 4 serving bowls and serve immediately.

Sen Mee Pad Prik Haeng

FRIED NOODLES WITH PORK AND CURRY PASTE

The quantity of curry paste to use in the recipe is up to you, according to your taste. Any remaining paste should be stored in an airtight container in the refrigerator for up to 7 days.
Serves 4

For the curry paste
5 large dried red chiles, seeded and coarsely chopped
1 teaspoon salt
1 teaspoon peeled and finely chopped galangal
1 tablespoon finely chopped lemongrass
3 tablespoons finely chopped garlic
3 tablespoons finely chopped shallots
1 tablespoon coriander seed
1 teaspoon cumin seed

For the fried noodles
2 tablespoons vegetable oil
2 garlic cloves, finely chopped
1 tablespoon curry paste
½ pound lean pork, thinly sliced
10 ounces rice vermicelli noodles, soaked in warm water for 5 minutes, rinsed under cold water, and drained
1¼ cups coarsely chopped celery
1¼ cups fresh bean sprouts
3 tablespoons fish sauce
2 tablespoons light soy sauce
1 teaspoon sugar

1 To make the curry paste, place the chiles in a mortar and pound them well, then add all the remaining ingredients in turn, pounding continuously to form a thick paste.
2 For the noodles, heat the oil in a wok and stir-fry the garlic until golden, then add the curry paste and stir well. Add the pork and stir-fry until it is cooked through, then add all the remaining ingredients, one by one in the above order, stirring after each addition, and cook until the noodles are soft. Transfer to a large dish and serve.

Pad Mi Sue

FRIED EGG NOODLES WITH PORK AND DRIED SHRIMP

This dish is popular for big parties as it can be served hot, but still tastes good when cold.
Serves 4

3 tablespoons vegetable oil
2¼ ounces dried shrimp
½ pound pork tenderloin, finely sliced
4 bunches egg noodles, cooked according to the package directions and drained

½ pound Chinese or regular celery, cut into thin sticks
2 tablespoons fish sauce
1 tablespoon oyster sauce

1 Heat the oil in a wok and stir-fry the dried shrimp until golden and crispy. Remove from the oil and set aside.
2 Stir-fry the pork until just cooked, then add the noodles and all the remaining ingredients, one by one in the above order, stirring well after each addition.
3 Add the crispy shrimp and stir well, then transfer to a warm platter and serve.

THAILAND Ba-Mee Moo Daeng

EGG NOODLES WITH BARBECUED PORK

In Thai, moo means pork, a fact that has amused and confused many foreigners. Daeng, meanwhile, means red. After you have barbecued the pork, if you have any left, it will keep in the refrigerator for about a week and is delicious served with rice or fried noodles.
Serves 4

For the barbecued pork
1 pound boneless pork loin chops
10 garlic cloves, crushed
1 tablespoon finely chopped cilantro root
1 teaspoon ground white pepper
2 tablespoons sugar
3 tablespoons light soy sauce
½ teaspoon red food coloring

For the noodles
4 bunches fresh egg noodles
2¼ cups fresh bean sprouts
¼ cup fish sauce
2 teaspoons sugar
¼ cup fresh lemon juice
¼ cup garlic oil
3 scallions, finely chopped

1 Place all the ingredients for the barbecued pork in a large bowl, cover, and let marinate in the refrigerator for 3 hours. Grill the pork until cooked through, then slice it thinly.
2 Shake the bunches of noodles to free the individual strands. Bring a pan of water to a boil and, using a strainer, dip the noodles in the boiling water for a few seconds until just soft, then rinse under cold running water and drain.
3 Turn the noodles into a large bowl and mix in all the remaining ingredients, except the scallions. Divide the noodle mixture among 4 serving bowls. Place the barbecued pork on top of the noodles, garnish with the scallions, and serve.

SPICY PORK NOODLES
WITH KAFFIR LIME LEAVES

*This dish was imported
to Thailand from China
and adapted to Thai
tastes with the addition
of chiles and kaffir lime
leaves, giving it a much
sharper, spicier taste
and making it a true
Thai specialty.*
Serves 4

2 tablespoons vegetable oil
3 garlic cloves, finely chopped
2 red chiles, finely chopped
½ pound lean pork, finely sliced
2 tablespoons fish sauce
1 tablespoon dark soy sauce
1 teaspoon sugar
2 medium tomatoes, thickly sliced

4 kaffir lime leaves, finely shredded
10 ounces flat rice stick noodles,
    soaked in warm water for
    5 minutes, rinsed under cold
    water, and drained
2 scallions, finely chopped

1 In a wok, heat the oil and stir-fry the garlic until golden. Add the chiles and stir for a few seconds, then add the pork and stir-fry until it is just cooked through.

2 Add the fish sauce, dark soy sauce, sugar, tomatoes, and kaffir lime leaves one by one, stirring after each addition.

3 Add the noodles and stir-fry briefly until they are cooked through. Transfer to a serving dish, garnish with the scallions, and serve.

HOT AND SOUR NOODLE SALAD

*The lettuce wraps
indicate that this recipe
has been influenced
by the Vietnamese
people who have
settled in Thailand.*
Serves 4

For the dipping sauce
1 cup white vinegar
4 tablespoons sugar
2 tablespoons salt
6 small red chiles
2 tablespoons pickled garlic,
    finely chopped
½ pound rice vermicelli noodles,
    cooked according to the package
    instructions, drained, and cut
    into 2-inch lengths

½ pound pork belly, boiled and cut
    into bite-size pieces
2 small Thai cucumbers, cut into
    thin sticks
1 small carrot, cut into thin sticks
1 tablespoon mint leaves
20 crisp lettuce leaves

1 In a pan, heat the vinegar, sugar, salt, and ¼ cup water until the mixture boils and thickens. Add the chiles and pickled garlic, mix thoroughly, then remove from the heat and let cool.

2 Wrap the vermicelli, pork, cucumber, carrot, and mint leaves in the lettuce leaves, place on a platter, and serve with the dipping sauce.

SHREDDED PORK AND NOODLE SOUP

This dish is eaten at any time of day in China, but can also be served as a soup course as part of a larger meal. If Chinese rice wine is not available, you can substitute a dry sherry.
Serves 4

4 dried Chinese black (shiitake) mushrooms, soaked in warm water for
    30 minutes
½ pound lean pork, shredded
1 tablespoon light soy sauce
1 tablespoon Chinese rice wine
1 teaspoon sugar
1 teaspoon cornstarch
¾ pound egg noodles
3 tablespoons vegetable oil
3 scallions, cut into 1-inch lengths
¾ cup canned, drained sliced bamboo shoots, shredded
½ teaspoon salt
2½ cups boiling chicken stock

1 Drain the mushrooms and squeeze them dry, retaining the liquid. Discard the stems, then slice the caps into thin strips.
2 Place the pork in a bowl with the soy sauce, rice wine, sugar, and cornstarch, and stir well. Cover and let marinate in a cool place for 20 minutes.
3 Meanwhile, cook the noodles in boiling water for 5 minutes, or according to the package directions, then drain.
4 Heat half the oil in a wok, add the marinated pork, and stir-fry until it changes color, then remove and set aside.
5 Drain the wok, heat the remaining oil in it, and add the scallions, mushrooms, and bamboo shoots. Stir, add the salt, then return the pork to the wok together with the reserved mushroom liquid.
6 Place the noodles in a large bowl and pour the boiling stock over, then add the pork and vegetables from the wok. Serve immediately.

NOODLES WITH PORK AND EGGS

When I was in Cambodia I noticed that when I saw this dish served, the egg yolks were very bright orange. I asked why, only to discover they were duck eggs. Luckily, the recipe works just as well with regular hen's eggs.

Serves 4

4 tablespoons vegetable oil

10 ounces flat rice stick noodles, soaked in warm water for 10 minutes, rinsed under cold water, and drained

1 tablespoon dark soy sauce

2 eggs

4 garlic cloves, finely chopped

10 ounces pork tenderloin, thinly sliced

2 tablespoons fish sauce

1 tablespoon light soy sauce

1 teaspoon sugar

6 tablespoons vegetable stock (see page 19)

2 cups coarsely chopped broccoli

1 tablespoon cornstarch, mixed with 4 tablespoons cold water

½ teaspoon ground black pepper

1 In a wok, heat 1 tablespoon of the oil and stir-fry the noodles for 2 minutes. Add the dark soy sauce and stir-fry for another 2 minutes. Turn the noodles onto a serving dish.

2 In a skillet, heat another 1 tablespoon of the oil and lightly fry 1 egg, then set it aside and keep warm.

3 Heat the remaining 2 tablespoons oil in the wok, add the garlic, and stir-fry until golden brown, then add the pork and stir-fry until it is just cooked through. Break in the remaining egg and stir it well into the mix.

4 One by one, add the fish sauce, light soy sauce, sugar, vegetable stock, and broccoli, stirring after each addition. When the broccoli is cooked al dente, add the cornstarch mixture to the pan and cook, stirring, until the sauce thickens. Pour the mixture over the noodles, top with the fried egg and black pepper, and serve.

CHOW MEIN

Chow mein *was one of the first Chinese dishes to become well known in the West. The term simply means fried noodles, and there are many different recipes. This is a traditional Chinese recipe.*
Serves 4

4 tablespoons peanut oil
4 bunches egg noodles, cooked according to the package directions, drained, and left to dry
1 garlic clove, finely chopped
½ teaspoon peeled and finely grated fresh ginger
½ pound roasted pork, cut into thin strips
½ pound skinless chicken breast fillet, blanched and cut into thin strips
3¼ cups thinly shredded white cabbage
1¼ cups fresh bean sprouts
6 scallions, cut into 2-inch lengths
8-ounce can sliced bamboo shoots, drained and cut into thin strips
⅔ cup chicken stock or water
2 tablespoons light soy sauce
2 teaspoons cornstarch, mixed with 2 tablespoons cold water

1 Heat 2 tablespoons of the oil in a large wok and stir-fry the noodles over medium heat until golden brown, then transfer to a large warmed dish and set aside.
2 Heat the remainder of the oil in the wok and stir-fry the garlic and ginger for 10 seconds, then add the pork and chicken and stir-fry for 2 minutes. Add the cabbage, bean sprouts, scallions, and bamboo shoots, stirring continuously.
3 Add the stock or water and soy sauce and bring to a boil. Add the cornstarch mixture and cook, stirring, until the sauce thickens. Pour over the noodles and serve.

Chow mein *was one of the first Chinese dishes to become well known in the West.*

FRIED EGG NOODLES WITH MIXED MEATS

This dish used to be served to impress people, by showing that the host could afford all the different ingredients, in particular the various types of meat.
Serves 4

For the marinade
¼ pound lean pork, finely sliced
¼ pound skinless chicken breast fillet, finely sliced
¼ pound raw medium shrimp, peeled and deveined
2 tablespoons oyster sauce
1 tablespoon sesame oil
1 tablespoon Chinese rice wine
2 garlic cloves, finely chopped
½ teaspoon ground white pepper

For the noodles
2 tablespoons vegetable oil
3 garlic cloves, finely chopped
4 bunches egg noodles, cooked according to the package directions, rinsed under cold water, and drained
4 dried wood ear (cloud ear) mushrooms, soaked in warm water for 30 minutes, drained, stems discarded, and finely sliced
2 tablespoons light soy sauce
2 tablespoons fish sauce
½ teaspoon sugar
1¾ cups bean sprouts
4 scallions, cut into 2-inch lengths

1 Place all the ingredients for the marinade in a bowl and mix well. Cover and let marinate in the refrigerator for 1 hour.
2 In a wok, heat the oil and stir-fry the garlic until golden, then add the marinade mixture and stir-fry briefly until the meats and shrimp start to change color.
3 Add the noodles and mushrooms and stir well. Then add all the remaining ingredients and cook, stirring quickly, until the meats and shrimp are cooked through. Transfer to a platter and serve.

NOODLES WITH STIR-FRIED GROUND PORK

Seasonings made from fermented soybeans are one of the oldest known food flavorings. The sweet paste in this recipe is a dark brown sauce with a rich salty-sweet flavor.

Serves 4

4 tablespoons sweet soybean paste

2 tablespoons light soy sauce

½ teaspoon sugar

½ teaspoon peeled and finely chopped fresh ginger

½ cup vegetable oil

10½ ounces ground pork

2 tablespoons dried shrimp, soaked in warm water for 10 minutes and finely chopped

2 cups chopped white cabbage

2 tablespoons peas, fresh or frozen (thawed if frozen)

½ teaspoon salt

2 scallions, finely sliced

1 pound fresh noodles, cooked according to the package directions, rinsed briefly under cold water, and drained

½ small cucumber, shredded

2 eggs, scrambled

1 cup fresh bean sprouts, blanched for 1 minute and drained

1 Mix together the soybean paste, soy sauce, sugar, and ginger, and set aside.

2 In a wok, heat 5 tablespoons of the vegetable oil and stir-fry the ground pork and dried shrimp for 30 seconds. Then add the cabbage, 1 cup water, peas, and salt, and stir-fry for another 2 minutes. Remove and set aside.

3 In the wok, heat the remaining oil, stir in the scallions, and stir-fry for 10 seconds. Return the meat and shrimp mixture to the pan, stir-fry for another 10 seconds, then add the sauce mixture and stir-fry over high heat for 1 minute. Remove to a bowl.

4 Divide the noodles among 4 serving bowls, place 2 or 3 tablespoons of the meat mixture over them, then top with the cucumber, scrambled eggs, and bean sprouts.

5 Mix thoroughly with chopsticks before eating.

Seasonings made from fermented soybeans are one of the oldest known food flavorings.

SPICY VERMICELLI SOUP WITH PORK AND FISHBALLS

In Thai tom means
to boil a liquid, yam
means spicy mixed
food, and wunsen
means vermicelli.
The combination of
pork and fish may be
unfamiliar to some
Westerners, but people
from Portugal and its
former colonies are
thoroughly at home
with it.
Serves 4

½ pound pork tenderloin
1 tablespoon vegetable oil
2 garlic cloves, finely chopped
1 quart chicken stock
16 Fishballs (see page 63)
3 tablespoons fish sauce
1 teaspoon sugar
1 teaspoon chili powder

½ pound mung bean vermicelli
  noodles, soaked in warm water
  for 10 minutes, rinsed under cold
  water, and drained
1¼ cups fresh bean sprouts
4 tablespoons ground roasted
  peanuts
2 scallions, finely chopped
1 lime, quartered

1 In a pan of boiling water, simmer the pork for 5 minutes, then drain, thinly slice, and set it aside.

2 In a wok, heat the oil and stir-fry the garlic until golden, remove from the heat, and set aside, reserving both garlic and oil.

3 Place the stock in a pan and bring to a boil. Add the fishballs, fish sauce, sugar, and chili powder, and bring back to a boil.

4 Divide the noodles, pork and bean sprouts among 4 serving bowls, then pour the stock mixture over. Garnish with the peanuts and scallions and a little of the garlic and oil, and serve with the lime quarters.

FRIED RICE NOODLES WITH ROAST PORK

Siam is the old
name for Thailand,
but in fact this
recipe is found
only in Singapore
and Malaysia.
Serves 4

3 tablespoons peanut oil
2 red onions, coarsely chopped
2 garlic cloves, crushed
½ pound roasted pork, cut into
  strips
2 red chiles, finely chopped
1 egg, lightly beaten
10½ ounces rice noodles, cooked
  according to the package
  directions and drained

1 tablespoon oyster sauce
2 tablespoons light soy sauce
2 tablespoons dark soy sauce
1¼ cups fresh bean sprouts
2 tomatoes, cut into eighths
3 scallions, chopped

1 Heat the oil in a wok and stir-fry the onions until they start to brown. Add the garlic and stir well, then add the pork and chiles and stir-fry for 2 minutes.

2 Add the egg and stir well. Then add the noodles and stir constantly until they are warmed through.

3 Add the oyster sauce and both soy sauces, stirring well, then the bean sprouts and tomatoes. Stir, transfer to a warmed dish, sprinkle with the scallions, and serve.

VERMICELLI AND GROUND PORK SOUP

Ron means hot in Thai, and vermicelli retain heat better than other kinds of noodle. Clear vermicelli noodles, often known as glass or cellophane noodles, are thin, translucent, and always sold dried.
Serves 4

2 cilantro roots, washed and finely chopped (available in Asian markets)
2 garlic cloves, finely chopped
½ teaspoon ground black pepper
3½ ounces ground pork
2 tablespoons fish sauce

1 medium onion, sliced
3½ ounces dried vermicelli noodles, soaked in warm water for 10 minutes, rinsed under cold water, and drained
1 egg, lightly beaten
2 scallions, finely chopped

1 Place the chopped cilantro root and garlic, together with the pepper, in a large mortar and pound to a paste, then add the pork and continue pounding until the consistency is smooth. Shape the mixture into 10 to 12 balls about ½ inch in diameter.
2 Bring 5 cups water to a boil in a pan, drop in the pork balls, and cook for 5 minutes, stirring continuously.
3 Add the fish sauce, onion, and noodles, simmer for a few minutes, then slowly stir in the egg. Remove from the heat.
4 Pour into a warmed tureen, sprinkle with the scallions, and serve.

Clear vermicelli noodles, often known as glass or cellophane noodles, are thin, translucent, and always sold dried.

RICE NOODLES WITH PORK AND BLACK BEAN SAUCE

Black bean sauce is made from fermented black soybean mash and can be found at most Asian markets. It has a delicious savory flavor and coats the other ingredients very nicely.
Serves 4

4 tablespoons vegetable oil
½ pound rice vermicelli noodles, soaked in warm water for 5 minutes, rinsed under cold water, and drained
1 teaspoon dark soy sauce
3 garlic cloves, finely chopped
½ pound lean pork, finely sliced
1 tablespoon black bean sauce
2 tablespoons fish sauce
1 cup pork stock
1 teaspoon cornstarch, mixed with 4 tablespoons cold water
½ pound Chinese or regular broccoli, finely sliced
1 teaspoon sugar
½ teaspoon ground white pepper

1 In a wok, heat 2 tablespoons of the oil, add the noodles, and stir quickly, then add the soy sauce and stir well. Transfer to a serving dish.
2 Add the remaining 2 tablespoons oil to the wok, add the garlic, and stir-fry until golden. Add the pork and stir-fry for 1 minute.
3 One by one, add the black bean sauce, fish sauce, pork stock, cornstarch mixture, broccoli, sugar, and white pepper, stirring well after each addition. Stir-fry until the pork is cooked through, then transfer to the noodles and serve.

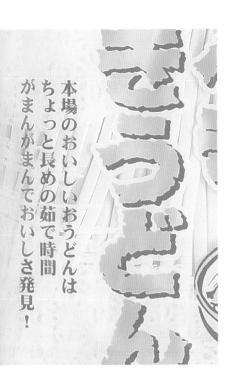

SINGAPORE FRIED NOODLES

The mixture of Chinese and Indian ingredients in this dish reflects the Singaporean cultural mix.

Serves 4

3 tablespoons vegetable oil

2 garlic cloves, crushed

¾-inch piece fresh ginger, peeled and finely chopped

1 small red chile, chopped into small pieces

¼ pound raw medium shrimp, peeled and deveined

5 small squid, cleaned and sliced into thin rings

2½ cups fresh bean sprouts

½ pound barbecued pork, cut into ½-inch cubes

2 eggs, beaten

½ pound rice vermicelli noodles, soaked in warm water for 5 minutes, rinsed briefly under cold water, and drained

3 scallions, finely chopped

2 tablespoons fish sauce

2 tablespoons hot curry powder

1 tablespoon light soy sauce

1 teaspoon sugar

1 Heat the oil in a wok, stir-fry the garlic, ginger, and chile together for 30 seconds, then add the shrimp and squid and stir-fry for 1 minute.

2 Add the bean sprouts and pork, and stir-fry for 2 minutes.

3 Make a well in the center of the mixture and pour in the eggs, scramble them lightly, then quickly mix in the noodles. Add all the remaining ingredients and stir until all the sauce is absorbed. Divide among 4 serving bowls and serve.

The mixture of Chinese and Indian ingredients in this dish reflects the Singaporean cultural mix.

Wet Tha Khauk-Swe-Gyaw

FRIED NOODLES WITH PORK AND DRIED CHILE

Dried red chiles are either soaked before being ground into a paste or just chopped to make chile flakes. They can also be dry ground to make roasted chili powder.

Serves 4

¼ cup peanut oil

4 garlic cloves, finely chopped

2 large dried red chiles, coarsely chopped

10 ounces pork tenderloin, thinly sliced

10 ounces flat rice stick noodles, soaked in warm water for 10 minutes, rinsed under cold water, and drained

1¼ cups small cauliflower florets

1 cup thinly sliced carrots

2 tablespoons fish sauce

2 tablespoons light soy sauce

½ teaspoon sugar

3 scallions, sliced into thin sticks

1 Heat the oil in a wok and stir-fry the garlic until golden. Add the chiles and stir-fry briefly, then add the pork and stir-fry until almost cooked through.

2 Add the noodles and stir quickly, then add the cauliflower and carrots in turn, stirring once after each addition.

3 Add the fish sauce, soy sauce, and sugar, and stir briefly. Finally, add the scallions, stir quickly, and serve.

Mee Pad Ham

STIR-FRIED NOODLES WITH HAM

I first had this dish in one of the large Chinese restaurants in Bangkok. Cured ham has been used for thousands of years in China.

Serves 4

3 tablespoons vegetable oil

2 garlic cloves, finely chopped

½ pound cooked ham, cut into strips

4 shiitake mushrooms, finely sliced

4 bunches egg noodles, cooked according to the package directions and drained

2 tablespoons light soy sauce

1 tablespoon oyster sauce

1 teaspoon sugar

2 tablespoons fish sauce

1¾ cups fresh bean sprouts

4 scallions, finely chopped

1 In a wok, heat the oil and stir-fry the garlic until golden, then add the ham and mushrooms and stir well.

2 Add the noodles and all the remaining ingredients one by one in the above order, stirring after each addition. Mix well, transfer to a serving platter, and serve.

BEEF Noodles

Bangkok used to be known as "The Venice of the East." The city was built along both sides of the great Chaopryah river, with many people living on the riverside or in houses built to float on the water. Until recently there were many canals or "klongs" that crossed the city. Traveling along them by boat was the standard way to get around. Even today, commuting to central Bangkok by taxi boat is completely normal, and although many of the canals have been filled in to make roads, a significant number are still there underneath them.

When I was a young boy there were small boats that each specialized in selling a certain food product, which might be cooked foods, noodles, coffee, or candy. My parents' house backed onto the Sathorn canal. The many noodle boats would announce themselves by honking their horns, whereupon we would run down the garden to buy from them.

Many of these boats became famous and noodle boats can still be found at the celebrated floating markets that still flourish around Bangkok. I have seen similar floating markets in Vietnam, on the Mekong River in the fertile Can Tho province. There are also several floating markets around Inle Lake in the hills of the Shan State in Burma.

As in Bangkok, trading starts before dawn, finishes by ten in the morning, and then starts up again in the late afternoon to avoid the fierce daytime heat. Boat noodles are sold in small, cheap portions, so people often order several different dishes to make up a meal. It's a very good way to experience a broad selection of tastes.

JAPANESE NOODLES WITH BEEF AND VEGETABLES

Miso is a staple of Japanese cuisine, made from the fermentation of soybeans or grains with salt and fungus. There are many different types, with a wide range of flavors.
Serves 4

14 ounces udon noodles
2 cups coarsely chopped green cabbage
1⅓ cups green beans, cut into 2-inch lengths
2 tablespoons sunflower oil
½ pound rump steak, sliced diagonally into bite-size pieces
1 small red bell pepper, seeded and cut into bite-size pieces
10 shiitake mushrooms, quartered
½ teaspoon salt
½ teaspoon chili powder
2 tablespoons red miso paste
2 tablespoons Japanese soy sauce
2 tablespoons sweet rice wine
1 scallion, finely sliced

1 Bring a large pan of water to a boil, add the noodles, and cook for 10 minutes, or according to the package directions. Drain, rinse under cold water, drain again, and then set aside.
2 Blanch the cabbage and beans for 2 minutes, then briefly refresh under cold water.
3 Heat the oil in a wok and stir-fry the beef for 2 minutes, then add the cabbage, beans, bell pepper, mushrooms, salt, and chili powder, and stir-fry for another 2 to 3 minutes.
4 In a bowl, mix together the miso, soy sauce, and rice wine, then add this mixture and the noodles to the wok and stir-fry for a minute.
5 Divide the mixture among 4 serving bowls, garnish with the scallion, and serve.

COLD NOODLE SOUP

The Korean name for this dish literally translates as "cold noodles." Originally from the region now known as North Korea, this dish has become extremely popular as a summer dish throughout South Korea as well.
Serves 4

1 pound thin rice noodles
½ pound cooked beef top round, cut into slices 2 inches by ½ inch
3½ cups beef stock
8 whole black peppercorns
2-inch piece fresh ginger, peeled
1 teaspoon salt
1 teaspoon soy sauce
4 dried chiles

To garnish
20 cucumber slices
1 large hard pear, peeled, cored, and thinly sliced
2 hard-boiled eggs, shelled and halved lengthwise

1 Cook the noodles in boiling water for 3 to 5 minutes, or according to the package directions, drain, rinse under cold running water, then drain again. Set aside to cool.
2 Put all the remaining ingredients in a pan, bring to a boil, and simmer for 5 minutes. Remove from the heat and let cool, then remove the peppercorns, ginger, and chiles.
3 Divide the noodles among 4 small serving bowls, then place the cucumber and pear slices in alternating layers over them. In each bowl, place an egg half on top, then carefully pour the cold soup over. Add a little Korean mustard and rice vinegar to taste, and serve.

The Korean name for this dish literally translates as "cold noodles."

STIR-FRIED NOODLES WITH BEEF, GINGER, AND SCALLIONS

Oyster sauce is a thick sauce used in many Chinese and Southeast Asian stir-fry recipes. To make it, oysters are boiled down in brine or water and combined with butter and seasonings to produce a rich, dark brown creamy sauce.

Serves 6

4 garlic cloves, finely chopped

1 pound beef tenderloin, thinly sliced

1 tablespoon cornstarch

1 egg

1 tablespoon oyster sauce

2 tablespoons peanut oil

1 tablespoon peeled and finely chopped fresh ginger

10 ounces rice stick noodles, soaked in warm water for 5 minutes, rinsed under cold water, and drained

2 tablespoons fish sauce

5 scallions, cut into 2-inch lengths

1 red bell pepper, seeded and cut into thin strips

1 In a bowl, place the garlic, beef, cornstarch, egg, and oyster sauce, and stir well. Cover and let marinate in a cool place for 30 minutes.

2 Heat the oil in a wok and stir-fry the ginger briefly, then add the marinated beef and stir-fry until it is just cooked through.

3 Add the noodles and stir-fry for 1 minute, then add the fish sauce, scallions, and bell pepper one by one, stirring briefly after each addition. Divide among individual serving bowls and serve.

Oyster sauce is a thick sauce used in many Chinese and Southeast Asian stir-fry recipes.

RICE VERMICELLI WITH MEATBALLS

Almondigas, or bola-bola, is the Filipino name for meatballs —somehow the "b" of the Spanish original has changed to an "m." Similar recipes can be found all over the world, sometimes served with rice noodles and sometimes with pasta. Serves 4

For the meat

1 pound ground beef

1 egg

3 tablespoons soft bread crumbs

½ teaspoon salt

½ teaspoon ground black pepper

4 garlic cloves, finely chopped

1 tablespoon all-purpose flour

2 tablespoons peanut oil

2 tomatoes, skinned and diced

2 cups beef stock

2 tablespoons dark soy sauce

2 scallions, finely chopped

For the noodles

10½ ounces rice vermicelli noodles, soaked in warm water for 5 minutes, rinsed in cold water, blanched briefly in boiling water, and drained

1 In a bowl, mix together the ground beef, egg, bread crumbs, salt, pepper, and half the garlic. Shape the mixture into balls and roll in the flour.

2 Heat the oil in a wok and stir-fry the balls until they are brown. Add the remaining garlic and the tomatoes, stir well, and cook gently until the tomatoes disintegrate. Now add the stock and soy sauce, and simmer for 10 minutes, turning the meatballs occasionally.

3 Transfer the meatballs and sauce to a warmed dish, sprinkle with the scallions, and serve with the noodles.

Almondigas, or bola-bola, *is the Filipino name for meatballs.*

PHILIPPINE FRIED NOODLES WITH MIXED MEAT AND VEGETABLES

Peanut oil is popular in Southeast Asia because it is inexpensive and can be reused, since it does not take on the taste of the food cooked in it. Pansit, or pancit as it is sometimes spelled, is probably the best-known Filipino dishes.

Serves 4

3 tablespoons peanut oil

1 small onion, finely chopped

½ pound skinless chicken fillets, cut into ½-inch cubes

½ pound pork, coarsely ground

¼ pound beef, coarsely ground

2½ cups coarsely chopped white cabbage

¼ pound raw medium shrimp, peeled and deveined

2 tablespoons light soy sauce

salt and pepper

½ pound thin rice noodles, cooked according to the package
    directions, rinsed under cold water, and drained

To garnish

2 hard-boiled eggs, shelled and quartered

1 small tomato, diced

cilantro leaves

1 In a small pan, heat 1 tablespoon of the oil and stir-fry the onion until golden. Set aside.

2 Heat the remaining 2 tablespoons oil in a wok and stir-fry the chicken, pork, and beef for 3 minutes. Stir in the cabbage and stir-fry for 2 minutes, then add the shrimp, soy sauce, and salt and pepper to taste. Stir well, then add the noodles a little at a time, stirring continuously.

3 Transfer to a warmed serving dish, garnish with the fried onions, hard-boiled eggs, tomato, and cilantro, and serve.

CURRY NOODLES WITH BEEF

Coming from the south of Thailand, this was originally a Muslim dish, probably originating in Malaysia.
Serves 4

2 tablespoons vegetable oil
2 garlic cloves, finely chopped
1 tablespoon red curry paste
1 cup coconut milk
¾ pound lean beef, cut into ½-inch cubes
2 teaspoons curry powder
3 tablespoons fish sauce
1 teaspoon sugar
½ pound rice stick noodles, soaked in warm water for 10 minutes, rinsed under cold water, and drained
2 hard-boiled eggs, shelled and quartered
2 tablespoons ground roasted peanuts

To garnish
4 ounces tofu, fried until crisp and thinly sliced
2 small shallots, finely sliced and fried until crisp and golden
2 scallions, finely sliced

1 In a wok, heat the oil and stir-fry the garlic for a few seconds. Add the curry paste and cook, stirring, for a few seconds, then add the coconut milk and stir well to mix.
2 Add the beef and stir well, then add 2 cups water and stir in the curry powder, fish sauce, and sugar. Cook for about 10 minutes.
3 Divide the noodles among 4 serving bowls and place 2 egg quarters on top of each portion of noodles.
4 Add the peanuts to the beef mixture, stir, then pour the mixture over the noodles. Garnish with the tofu, shallots, and scallions, and serve.

Coming from the south of Thailand, this recipe was a Muslim dish probably originating in Malaysia.

DANANG FRIED NOODLES WITH BEEF

Danang is a lovely Vietnamese seaside town, and this recipe is named after a meal I ate in a restaurant there one lunchtime.
Serves 4

3 tablespoons vegetable oil

1 medium onion, coarsely chopped

10 ounces beef tenderloin, thinly sliced

6 bunches egg noodles, cooked according to the package directions and drained

¾ cup dried wood ear (cloud ear) mushrooms, soaked in warm water for 20 minutes, drained, stems discarded, and sliced

1 celery stalk, chopped into ¾-inch slices

2 medium tomatoes, quartered, then halved

2 tablespoons fish sauce

1 tablespoon light soy sauce

1 teaspoon sugar

½ teaspoon ground white pepper

cilantro leaves, to garnish

1 Heat the oil in a wok and stir-fry the onion until transparent, then add the beef and stir-fry until almost cooked through.

2 Add all the remaining ingredients, one by one in the above order, stirring after each addition. When all the ingredients are in the wok, stir once, then transfer to a serving plate, garnish with cilantro leaves, and serve.

BEEF NOODLE SOUP WITH BASIL LEAVES

Laos and Thailand are separated only by the Mekong River, and the two cultures are very similar. I first ate this dish in Laos, but it is frequently served in Thailand too.
Serves 4

6 cups beef stock

2 tablespoons vegetable oil

3 garlic cloves, finely chopped

1¼ cups fresh bean sprouts

6 ounces fresh rice noodles

½ pound lean beef, cut into fine slivers

40 basil leaves, lightly crushed

1 Pour the stock into a large pan and bring to a boil, then set aside and keep warm.

2 In a small pan, heat the oil and fry the garlic until golden, then remove the pan from the heat and set aside.

3 Bring a large pan of water to a boil. Using a strainer, plunge the bean sprouts into the boiling water for a few seconds, then remove, drain, and turn into a large serving bowl.

4 Place the noodles in the strainer and dip in the boiling water for 10 seconds, drain, and turn into the large serving bowl with the bean sprouts.

5 Again using the strainer, plunge the beef into the boiling water, keeping it there until it is just cooked through, then remove, drain, and add to the serving bowl.

6 Add the reserved garlic and oil to the bowl with the bean sprouts and beef, stir together briefly, then pour the hot stock over, add the basil leaves, and serve.

RICE NOODLE SOUP WITH BEEF

Pho *is a well-known Vietnamese noodle dish. Believed to derive partly from French cuisine, it typifies the Asian habit of sharing dishes, with each diner eating several small portions but varying the contents and taste each time.*
Serves 4

1¾ pounds beef bones

14 ounces chuck steak

2 medium onions, sliced into rings

1 tablespoon peeled and coarsely grated fresh ginger

1 cinnamon stick, broken into 2-inch pieces

12 black peppercorns, crushed

salt

2 tablespoons fish sauce

8 red and green chiles, sliced into thin rings

2 limes or lemons, diced into small segments

5 scallions, cut into ¾-inch pieces

4 tomatoes, skinned, seeded, and cut into pieces

4 celery stalks, cut into thin strips

1¼ cups fresh bean sprouts

14 ounces lean roasting beef or top boneless sirloin steak, cut into paper-thin strips

4½ ounces rice vermicelli noodles, cooked according to the package directions and drained

1 Place the bones in a deep pan, together with the chuck steak, onions, ginger, cinnamon, and crushed peppercorns. Pour over at least 2 quarts water, to cover the ingredients. Bring to a boil, cover, and simmer for at least 4 hours, occasionally skimming the surface to remove any fat. Add salt to taste. Keep warm in the oven in an ovenproof bowl until serving.

2 Put the fish sauce, chiles, and lime or lemon in small bowls. Place the remaining vegetables, the bean sprouts, and the strips of beef on a serving dish. Reheat the vermicelli and place in a large bowl.

3 Set all the dishes on the table, together with the warm stock. Ladle some stock into each of the bowls. Add the vermicelli, then the meat and vegetables in small quantities to your own taste, let cook in the stock, and eat when ready.

FLAT BEEF NOODLES AND BLACK BEAN SAUCE

The root of the ginger plant, when used in cooking, must always be fresh so that it is tender and juicy.
Serves 4

4 tablespoons vegetable oil
¾ pound top boneless sirloin steak, thinly sliced
1-inch piece fresh ginger, peeled and finely chopped
2 garlic cloves, crushed
2 small red or green bell peppers, seeded and diced
5 scallions, chopped
10 ounces rice stick noodles, soaked in warm water for 5 minutes, rinsed briefly under cold water, and drained
2 tablespoons black bean sauce
2 tablespoons light soy sauce
2 tablespoons Chinese rice wine
1 teaspoon sugar

1 Heat 3 tablespoons of the vegetable oil in a wok and stir-fry the beef slices for 4 to 5 minutes, then stir in the ginger and garlic. Add the bell peppers and scallions, and stir-fry for 1 to 2 minutes.
2 Add the noodles, the remaining 1 tablespoon oil, the black bean and soy sauces, rice wine, and sugar, and stir until the noodles are well coated. Divide among 4 serving bowls and serve.

Daping Sapi Dan Mihun

BEEF WITH FRIED RICE VERMICELLI

Ginger is one of the most extensively used spices in Asian cooking. Try to buy the young roots, which are pinkish in color and have more flavor.

Serves 4

3 tablespoons peanut oil

2 small onions, chopped

4 garlic cloves, finely chopped

1 pound lean chuck beef, cut into ¾-inch cubes

2 teaspoons *sambal ulek* (see page 46)

2 cups beef stock

2 tablespoons sweet soy sauce

1 teaspoon cornstarch, mixed with 2 tablespoons cold water

2 tablespoons finely chopped chives

½ teaspoon ground ginger

½ teaspoon sugar

salt and pepper

¾ pound rice vermicelli

1 small cucumber, cut into thin sticks

2 tomatoes, skinned and sliced

1 Heat 2 tablespoons of the oil in a wok and stir-fry the onions until they are transparent. Add the garlic, then the beef, *sambal ulek*, and beef stock, stirring well. Cover the wok and simmer until the meat is tender, about 2 hours.

2 Add the soy sauce, then stir the cornstarch mixture into the wok. Cook gently, stirring, for a few minutes, then stir in the chives, ground ginger, sugar, and salt and pepper to taste. Set aside.

3 In a second wok or skillet, fry the vermicelli according to the package directions until golden, then drain and place in a warmed bowl. Cover with the cooked meat mixture, garnish with the cucumber and tomato slices, and serve.

Ginger is one of the most extensively used spices in Asian cooking.

SPICY BEEF NOODLES WITH YARD-LONG BEANS AND DRIED RED CHILES

Yard-long beans, also known as Chinese long beans or asparagus beans, are often available from Asian markets and some supermarkets, but can be expensive. They can easily be replaced with green beans.
Serves 4

3 tablespoons peanut oil
4 garlic cloves, finely chopped
2 large dried red chiles, sliced into small rings
½ pound beef tenderloin, thinly sliced
2 tablespoons fish sauce
1 tablespoon dark soy sauce
½ teaspoon sugar
¼ pound yard-long beans or green beans, chopped into 2-inch lengths
½ pound medium flat rice stick noodles, soaked in warm water for
    10 minutes, rinsed under cold water, and drained
cilantro leaves, to garnish

1 In a wok, heat the oil and stir-fry the garlic until golden. Add the chiles and stir twice.
2 Add the beef and stir well, then add the fish sauce, soy sauce, sugar, and beans. Stir-fry until the beans are tender, then add the noodles and stir-fry until they are cooked through.
3 Turn into a serving dish, garnish with cilantro leaves, and serve.

THAILAND   Gueyteow Pad Nua Mow

SPICY NOODLES WITH BEEF AND KAFFIR LIME LEAVES

Kaffir lime trees are grown extensively in Southeast Asia. The limes have a knobbly skin. Their juice can be used in cooking, but the leaves are a more important ingredient: fresh or dried, they are used to flavor soups and curries.
Serves 4

3 tablespoons vegetable oil
3 garlic cloves, finely chopped
3 small red chiles, finely chopped
5 kaffir lime leaves, finely sliced
10½ ounces beef tenderloin, cut
    into bite-size pieces
9 ounces rice stick noodles, cooked
    according to the package
    directions, rinsed under cold
    water, and drained

2 tablespoons fish sauce
2 tablespoons light soy sauce
1 tablespoon oyster sauce
1 teaspoon sugar
1 medium onion, coarsely chopped
2 medium tomatoes, cut into eighths

1 In a wok, heat the oil and stir-fry the garlic, chiles, kaffir lime leaves, and beef.
2 When the beef is just cooked, add the noodles, stirring continuously. Add all the remaining ingredients, one by one in the above order, stirring after each addition.
3 Mix well, turn into a large dish, and serve.

KOREAN BRAISED BEEF WITH NOODLES

Chili oil is made by the infusion of crushed dried red chiles in hot oil, creating a clear red oil often used as a condiment. It has a very hot flavor.

Serves 2

1½ pounds chuck steak

salt and pepper

1 pound scallions, cut into 1-inch lengths

1 teaspoon sugar

1 teaspoon chili oil

2 tablespoons peanut oil

¼ pound rice vermicelli, cooked according to the package directions, rinsed under cold water, and drained

2 eggs, beaten

1 Place the meat in a large pan, cover with water, and bring to a boil. Add a pinch of salt and pepper, then cover and simmer for 1 hour, skimming the surface from time to time. Allow the meat to cool, then shred it, leaving it in the liquid in the pan.

2 Reheat the pan containing the meat, adding the scallions, sugar, and chilli oil. Stir well until the sugar has dissolved and the mixture is hot.

3 Heat the peanut oil in a wok and cook the vermicelli until it is hot and starts to color, then remove it from the wok and stir it into the meat mixture in the pan.

4 Pour the eggs into the mixture, stirring lightly, then remove from the heat, pour into a large bowl, and serve.

CHINA Ng Hieng Joek Sie

NOODLES WITH BEEF IN FIVE-SPICE SAUCE

Dark soy sauce is thicker than the light variety. Both are generally available from Asian markets.

Serves 4

2 tablespoons peanut oil

3 garlic cloves, crushed

½ teaspoon salt

½ teaspoon peeled and grated fresh ginger

1 tablespoon dark soy sauce

1 teaspoon sugar

½ teaspoon five-spice powder

¾ pound lean beef, cut crosswise into thin slices, then into small squares

⅔ cup beef stock

1 teaspoon cornstarch

4 to 6 bunches egg noodles, cooked according to the package directions, drained, and fried

1 Heat the oil in a wok, add the garlic, salt, ginger, soy sauce, sugar, and five-spice powder, and stir until the sugar has dissolved.

2 Mix the beef into the mixture and let stand for 10 to 15 minutes, then add the stock and bring to a boil.

3 Mix the cornstarch with 1 tablespoon cold water, stir into the mixture, and cook, stirring continuously, until the sauce has thickened. Pour over the fried noodles and serve.

NOODLE SOUP WITH MEATBALLS

Bakso or baso *is a ball made from meat, fish, shrimp, or tofu, or a combination of the four ingredients.*
Serves 4 to 6

For the meatballs
½ pound lean beef, finely ground, then chopped to form a paste
3 tablespoons cornstarch
1 egg white
white pepper and salt
1 teaspoon sea salt

For the soup
3½ ounces egg noodles
½ teaspoon salt
2 tablespoons vegetable oil
3 shallots, finely sliced
2 garlic cloves, finely sliced
1 tablespoon light soy sauce
1½ quarts beef stock
4 scallions, finely sliced into rounds
2 medium carrots, sliced into rounds
3 Chinese (napa) cabbage leaves, sliced

1 To make the meatballs, place the beef paste in a bowl with the cornstarch and egg white, and season with salt and pepper. Mix well, then shape into balls about ½ inch in diameter. Drop the meatballs into a bowl of water with the sea salt added.
2 In a pan, bring 2½ cups water to a boil, remove the meatballs from the salted water, and drop them into the boiling water. Cook for 5 to 8 minutes, drain, and set aside.
3 To make the soup, bring a large pan of water to a boil, add the noodles and salt, and boil for 5 minutes. Drain and rinse under cold running water, then drain again and set aside.
4 Heat the oil in a large pan, add the shallots and garlic, and stir-fry for 1 minute. Add the soy sauce, stock, scallions, and carrots, and simmer for 5 minutes, then add the cabbage leaves and simmer for another 4 minutes.
5 Add the noodles and meatballs, increase the heat, and cook for another minute, then serve immediately.

Bakso or baso *is a ball made from meat, fish, shrimp, or tofu, or a combination of the four.*

STIR-FRIED NOODLES WITH BEEF AND BAMBOO SHOOTS

Sesame grows extensively in Asia and the seed is frequently used in cooking. It has a nutty taste and is quite oily.
Serves 4

3 tablespoons vegetable oil
2 garlic cloves, finely chopped
10½ ounces beef tenderloin, thinly sliced
½ pound rice stick noodles, soaked in warm water for 20 minutes,
   rinsed under cold water, and drained
1¾ cups canned, drained sliced bamboo shoots, cut into thin strips
4 scallions, finely sliced
¼ cup fish sauce
4 tablespoons sesame seeds, lightly toasted

1 Heat the oil in a wok and fry the garlic and the beef, stirring well. Add the noodles and stir, then add the bamboo shoots and scallions and stir-fry for 3 minutes.
2 Add the fish sauce and 3 tablespoons water, then stir in half the sesame seed. Transfer to a large dish, sprinkle with the remaining sesame seeds, and serve.

RICE VERMICELLI WITH BEEF AND BEANS

The yard-long bean or Chinese long bean is common all over China and Southeast Asia. It can be up to a yard long, resembling an overgrown green bean. It is very crunchy and cooks quickly.
Serves 4

2 tablespoons peanut oil
1 tablespoon sesame oil
½ pound yard-long beans or green beans, cut into 2-inch lengths
2 garlic cloves, finely chopped
½ teaspoon peeled and grated fresh ginger
¾ pound top round or top boneless sirloin steak, cut into strips
2/3 cup beef stock
2 tablespoons light soy sauce
½ pound rice vermicelli noodles, cooked according to the package
   directions and drained

1 Heat 1 tablespoon of the peanut oil and ½ tablespoon of the sesame oil in a wok and stir-fry the beans for 2 minutes. Remove from the wok with a skimmer, leaving them to drain over the wok for a few moments, then set aside.
2 Add the remaining 1 tablespoon peanut oil and ½ tablespoon sesame oil to the wok and stir-fry the garlic and ginger for 30 seconds. Add the strips of beef and stir-fry until the meat changes color, then push the meat to the side of the wok. Add the stock and soy sauce, stirring well, then add the noodles and cook gently for 2 minutes.
3 Return the meat and beans to the pan, stir-fry until hot, and serve.

PEKING-STYLE BEEF FRIED NOODLES

Chinese people refer to Peking as being "the real China," and this recipe is certainly authentically Chinese.
Serves 4

1 pound fresh flat wheat noodles
¼ cup vegetable oil
1 medium onion, coarsely chopped
2 slices peeled fresh ginger, finely chopped
2 garlic cloves, finely chopped
½ pound ground beef
½ teaspoon salt
1 tablespoon yellow bean paste
1 tablespoon light soy sauce
¼ cup beef stock
1 tablespoon cornstarch
1 small cucumber, cut into thin sticks
2 scallions, cut into thin sticks

1 Prepare the noodles: dip them in boiling water for 15 seconds, or under just soft, then drain and place on a large serving dish.
2 Heat the vegetable oil in a wok and stir-fry the onion and ginger for 1 minute, then add the garlic and ground beef and stir-fry over medium heat for 3 minutes.
3 Add the salt, yellow bean paste, and soy sauce. Stirring well, cook for 3 minutes, then add the stock and cook for another 3 minutes.
4 Mix the cornstarch with ¼ cup cold water, add to the pan, and cook, stirring, until the mixture thickens, then pour over the noodles. Place the cucumber and scallions on top and serve.

Chinese people refer to Peking as being "the real China," and this recipe is authentically Chinese.

FISH AND SEAFOOD

During a trip to Indonesia I went to visit the famous temple at Borobodur on the island of Java. Built as a Buddhist temple around the ninth century, it later became a Hindu temple and was then abandoned for five hundred years. It was rediscovered in the nineteenth century hidden beneath jungle and ash from a nearby volcano. Restoration began forty years ago and is still ongoing.

As with other large temples, the dawn is considered the best time of day for a visit. I left my hotel around five in the morning and climbed the long stairway to the top of the temple. Watching the sun rise and seeing the color of the dawn sky was truly spectacular. I experienced a tremendous feeling of peace and an awareness of the spirituality of Buddhism. I also spent some time looking at the thousands of wonderful stone carvings that depict scenes from the life of the Buddha.

In contrast to Borobodur, the twelfth-century temple complex at Angkor Wat near Siem Reap in Cambodia was built as a Hindu temple and later became a Buddhist center. It too was abandoned—nobody is quite sure when—and rediscovered many hundreds of years later. The Angkor temple complex is famous for the quality of the stone carvings on its walls. Some of them depict the lives of the Hindu gods, while others chronicle the everyday life of Angkor, with people harvesting crops, fishing, and cooking. Apparently, the main cooking methods were grilling over open fires and boiling in water.

After Marco Polo's famous thirteenth-century journey to China, the theory arose that he took pasta to that country, creating the basis for noodles. It now seems more likely that things worked the other way round. Personally, I like to eat both pasta and noodles!

FRIED NOODLES WITH MIXED SEAFOOD

*Although this is a
Chinese recipe, it
is widely cooked in
Thailand. This was my
father's favorite dish,
and in my childhood
memories of the family
going out to eat, he
is always wolfing down
a plateful of this.*
Serves 4

4 tablespoons vegetable oil

4 bunches egg noodles, cooked according to the package directions,
    rinsed under cold water, and drained

3 garlic cloves, finely chopped

¼ pound squid, cleaned and cut into ½-inch rings

¼ pound raw medium shrimp, peeled and deveined

¼ pound lump crabmeat

2 tablespoons fish sauce

2 tablespoons oyster sauce

2 tablespoons Chinese rice wine

1 ounce fresh ginger, peeled and finely sliced

1¾ cups fresh bean sprouts

4 scallions, cut into 2-inch lengths

½ teaspoon sugar

½ teaspoon ground white pepper

1 cup vegetable stock (see page 19)

2 tablespoons cornstarch, mixed with ½ cup cold water

1 Heat 2 tablespoons of the oil in a large wok and stir-fry the noodles over medium
heat until they are golden, then remove from the wok, set aside, and keep warm.

2 Heat the remaining 2 tablespoons oil in the wok and stir-fry the garlic for 10 seconds.
Add all the remaining ingredients, except the stock and the cornstarch mixture, and
stir-fry for 2 minutes, or until the shrimp have just changed color, then add the stock
and cornstarch mixture and cook, stirring continuously, until the sauce thickens.

3 Place the noodles on a warmed platter, pour the seafood mixture over, and serve.

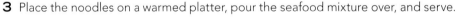

HUNAN NOODLES WITH TOFU AND CRAB SAUCE

When I visited Hunan I found the food spicier than in other regions of China. This dish is no exception.

Serves 4

3 tablespoons peanut oil
1 tablespoon black bean sauce
2 scallions, finely chopped
2 small red and green chiles, finely chopped
2 garlic cloves, finely chopped
6 ounces lump crabmeat
1 tablespoon light soy sauce

2/3 cup vegetable stock (see page 19)
2 blocks (4 inches square) firm tofu, cut into 3/4-inch cubes
9 ounces rice vermicelli noodles, cooked according to the package directions, drained, and set aside in a warmed dish

1 Heat the oil in a wok and add the black bean sauce, scallions, chiles, garlic, and crabmeat, stirring well.

2 Add the soy sauce, stock, and tofu cubes, stirring carefully. Simmer gently for 10 minutes, then spread the mixture over the noodles and serve.

STIR-FRIED NOODLES WITH CHINESE LEAVES AND SHRIMP

The term "Chinese leaves" here covers many different plants, among them bok choy, choy sum, and Chinese (napa) cabbage. I suggest you see which are available at your local Asian market. You can also use broccoli or cauliflower instead.

Serves 4

3 tablespoons peanut oil
3 garlic cloves, crushed
6 ounces raw medium shrimp, peeled and deveined
2 eggs, beaten
1/2 pound rice vermicelli noodles, soaked in warm water for 5 minutes, rinsed under cold water, and drained

1 small head bok choy, choy sum, or Chinese (napa) cabbage, thick stems discarded, and cut into finger-width strips
1 tablespoon fish sauce
1 tablespoon light soy sauce

1 Heat the oil in a wok and stir-fry the garlic for 30 seconds, then add the shrimp and stir-fry for 2 minutes.

2 Add the eggs and continue to stir-fry until they are set. Add the noodles, Chinese leaves, fish sauce, and soy sauce. Stir well, turn into a warmed dish, and serve.

EGG NOODLE AND SQUID SALAD

This is another of my family's favorite dishes. My mother loved cooking it.
Serves 4

4 bunches egg noodles
¾ pound squid, cleaned and coarsely chopped
2 cups coarsely chopped white cabbage
¼ cup fish sauce
2 tablespoons light soy sauce
1 teaspoon sugar
¼ cup fresh lemon juice
2 small red chiles, finely chopped
3 scallions, cut into 2-inch lengths

1 Bring a pan of water to a boil, add the noodles, and simmer until they soften and separate. Remove from the water, drain, and hold under cold running water to stop the cooking process. Drain well again and set aside.
2 Place the squid in a pan, cover with water, and bring to a boil. Remove from the water, drain, and set aside.
3 Dip the cabbage in the boiling water, drain, and set aside.
4 Place the noodles, squid, cabbage, and all the remaining ingredients in a bowl, and mix well. Divide among 4 serving bowls and serve.

GRILLED SHRIMP
WITH THIN RICE VERMICELLI

When you make this dish, grill the shrimp whole, as this gives a wonderful aroma. In Asia these shrimp would be served shell-on and peeled by the diner.
Serves 4

1 pound raw large or jumbo shrimp, shell-on
6 ounces thin rice vermicelli noodles
2 teaspoons vegetable oil
3 scallions, chopped into ¾-inch lengths
30 roasted peanuts

To garnish
1 lemon, thinly sliced
cilantro leaves

1 Grill the shrimp until they have completed changed color, turning once. When cool enough to handle, peel, devein, then cut each one in half and set aside.
2 In a large pan, bring 2 quarts water to a boil, add the noodles, and boil for 2 minutes. Drain, rinse under cold running water, then drain again and set aside.
3 Heat the oil in a skillet, add the scallions, and fry gently until softened.
4 Arrange the noodles on a warmed serving plate, place the shrimp on top of the noodles, then sprinkle the scallions and roasted peanuts over the top. Garnish with the lemon slices and cilantro leaves, and serve.

Grill the shrimp whole, as this gives a wonderful aroma.

Mi Bun Xao Voi Rac Dau

STIR-FRIED NOODLES WITH SQUID AND VEGETABLES

I first ate this dish in a Vietnamese community in Northeast Thailand, where the Vietnamese refugees settled after the Vietnam War.

Serves 4

1 tablespoon vegetable oil
2 garlic cloves, finely chopped
6 small squid, cleaned and sliced
1 carrot, thinly sliced
1 small head Chinese (napa) cabbage, shredded
1 celery stalk, finely sliced

¼ cup chicken stock
1 tablespoon oyster sauce
1 tablespoon fish sauce
½ pound rice vermicelli noodles, soaked in warm water for 5 minutes, rinsed under cold water, and drained

1 Heat the oil in a wok and stir-fry the garlic until golden brown, then add the squid and stir-fry for 1 minute.
2 Add all the remaining ingredients, except the noodles, and cook for another 2 minutes, stirring gently.
3 Add the noodles and stir well for 1 minute or until heated through, then serve.

THAILAND Tom Yam Kung

HOT AND SOUR NOODLE SOUP

This is one of the best-known dishes in Thai cuisine. Kaffir lime is sometimes called "wild lime." The skin and leaves are used frequently in Southeast Asian cooking.

Serves 4

4½ cups chicken stock
4 kaffir lime leaves, sliced
1 lemongrass stalk, cut into 2-inch lengths
4 small red chiles, crushed
12 raw large shrimp, peeled and deveined
⅓ cup fish sauce
1 tablespoon sugar

16 fresh straw mushrooms, halved
⅓ cup fresh lemon juice
7 ounces rice vermicelli, soaked in warm water for 3 minutes, rinsed under cold water, drained, and divided among 4 serving bowls
cilantro leaves, to garnish

1 In a pan, heat the chicken stock and add the kaffir lime leaves, lemongrass, and chiles. Bring to a boil and then simmer for 5 minutes.
2 Add the shrimp, fish sauce, sugar, and mushrooms, and simmer for another 3 minutes, stirring well.
3 Add the lemon juice, stir once, then pour over the noodles and garnish with cilantro.

THAILAND Ba Mee Nah Talay
EGG NOODLES WITH SEAFOOD

This dish is a big hit in my restaurant on the island of Ko Samui, where lots of fresh seafood is delivered every day by the local fishermen.
Serves 4

4 bunches egg noodles

4 tablespoons vegetable oil

4 garlic cloves, finely chopped

¼ pound raw medium shrimp, peeled and deveined

¼ pound baby squid, cut into ½-inch rings

¼ pound lump crabmeat

¾ cup canned, drained sliced bamboo shoots, cut into thin sticks

12 straw mushrooms, halved

2 tablespoons light soy sauce

1 tablespoon dark soy sauce

2 tablespoons fish sauce

½ teaspoon sugar

1 cup vegetable stock (see page 19)

1 tablespoon cornstarch, mixed with ¼ cup cold water

3 scallions, coarsely chopped

1 Take the bunches of noodles and shake them to separate the noodles. Bring a pan of water to a boil and, using a strainer, dip the noodles into the boiling water for a few seconds, then rinse under cold running water and drain.

2 In a wok, heat 2 tablespoons of the oil and stir-fry the noodles briefly until they start to darken, then divide among 4 serving plates.

3 Heat the remainder of the oil in the wok and fry the garlic until golden, then add the shrimp, squid, and crabmeat, and stir-fry until the shrimp and squid are just cooked. Add the bamboo shoots and mushrooms, stirring well, followed by the soy sauces, fish sauce, sugar, and stock in turn, stirring briefly after each addition.

4 Add the cornstarch mixture and cook, stirring continuously, until the sauce thickens, about 2 minutes. Add the scallions and stir, then transfer to the noodles and serve.

SHRIMP AND VERMICELLI HOTPOT

To cook this dish you need a clay pot or a heavy-bottomed pan. The original clay pots were glazed on the inside only and used for slow cooking, braising, and stewing. Serves 4

6 ounces mung bean vermicelli noodles, soaked in warm water for
   10 minutes, rinsed under cold water, and drained
4 dried Chinese black (shiitake) mushrooms, soaked in hot water for
   30 minutes, drained, stems discarded, and finely sliced
1 tablespoon peeled and finely chopped fresh ginger
3 scallions, cut into ¾-inch lengths
½ pound raw medium shrimp, peeled and deveined
1 tablespoon oyster sauce
1 tablespoon light soy sauce
½ teaspoon sugar
½ teaspoon ground black pepper
cilantro sprigs, to garnish

1 Place the ingredients, one by one in the above order, in layers in a clay pot or heavy-bottomed pan.

2 Cover and place over medium heat for 5 minutes. Check that the shrimp are cooked, then remove from the heat and serve, garnished with cilantro sprigs.

PRODUCT OF JAPAN

NET WT. 16 OZ. (1LB.) 453G

FISH RICE NOODLE SOUP

In Cambodia, this dish is normally served at breakfast. Why not try it as an alternative to your bowl of cereal? White turmeric, as its name suggests, is a lighter color than the regular deep orange roots—look for it in Asian markets.

Serves 4

1 whole fish (mackerel or sea bass), weighing about 3½ pounds, cleaned
3 tablespoons finely chopped fresh white turmeric
3 garlic cloves, peeled
3 lemongrass stalks, thinly sliced
2 tablespoons fish sauce
1 teaspoon sugar
1 cup coconut milk
½ pound medium rice vermicelli noodles
½ cup fresh bean sprouts
⅓ cup shredded cucumber
¾ cup shredded white cabbage

1 In a large pan, bring 1½ quarts water to a boil. Add the fish and bring back to the boil, then simmer for about 15 minutes or until the fish flakes easily. Remove the fish from the pan and set aside the liquid.

2 Remove the flesh from the fish and discard the skin and bones. Place the white turmeric, garlic, and lemongrass in a large mortar and grind them together with a pestle, then add the fish and grind all together into a smooth paste.

3 Bring the fish cooking liquid back to the boil, add the fish sauce, sugar, and coconut milk, and return to a boil. Add the fish mixture from the mortar and boil for another 10 minutes, then set aside.

4 In a large pan, bring 2 quarts water to a boil. Add the noodles and cook for 5 minutes. Drain, rinse under cold running water, and then drain again. Divide the vermicelli among 4 serving bowls, add the bean sprouts, cucumber, and cabbage, then ladle the hot soup over the top and serve.

FRIED NOODLES WITH RED SNAPPER AND SQUID

Sesame oil is a thick, aromatic oil made from crushed white sesame seed. It has a deliciously nutty flavor.
Serves 4

2 tablespoons vegetable oil
2 garlic cloves, finely chopped
2 eggs, lightly beaten
1lb 2 ounces fresh rice noodles
2 tablespoons light soy sauce
1 tablespoon dark soy sauce
½ cup chicken stock
2½ ounces red snapper fillet, sliced
1¾ ounces squid, cleaned and sliced
1¾ ounces raw medium shrimp, peeled and deveined
2 choy sum leaves, or collard green leaves, cut into 1¼-inch slices
¾ cup fresh bean sprouts
½ teaspoon white pepper
1 teaspoon sesame oil
salt

1 Heat the oil in a wok and sitr-fry the garlic for a few seconds until golden, then add the eggs and cook until they start to set.
2 Add the noodles and stir well, then add the soy sauces and stock. Bring the mixture to a boil, then add the fish, squid, and shrimp.
3 Cook over high heat until the seafood is cooked, then add the vegetables, pepper, and sesame oil. Season to taste with salt. Stir-fry over high heat for another minute, then serve.

FRIED EGG NOODLES WITH LOBSTER IN A PIQUANT SAUCE

The Chinese have been making wine for centuries using herbs, leaves, rice, and spices. If you can't get hold of rice wine, feel free to use dry sherry instead.
Serves 4

4 tablespoons peanut oil
4 bunches egg noodles, cooked according to the package directions, rinsed under cold water, and drained
2 garlic cloves, finely chopped
1 teaspoon peeled and finely chopped fresh ginger
1½ pounds lobster, peeled and the tails cut into pieces
1 red bell pepper, seeded and cut into ½-inch squares
2 tablespoons black bean sauce
1 cup chicken stock
2 tablespoons Chinese rice wine
1 egg, lightly beaten
2 tablespoons cornstarch, mixed with 2 tablespoons cold water
1 tablespoon sesame oil
2 tablespoons light soy sauce
4 scallions, cut into 2-inch lengths
ground white pepper

1 Heat 2 tablespoons of the oil in a large wok and stir-fry the noodles until browned. Remove from the heat and keep warm.
2 Heat the remaining 2 tablespoons oil in the wok and stir-fry the garlic and ginger for 10 seconds. Add the lobster meat and stir quickly, then add the bell pepper, black bean sauce, stock, and rice wine, stirring continuously
3 Bring the mixture to a boil, then slowly add the egg, stirring continuously to form threads in the sauce.
4 Add the cornstarch mixture and cook, stirring, until the sauce thickens. Add the sesame oil, soy sauce, and scallions, and cook for another 2 minutes, adding white pepper to taste. Transfer to a warmed platter and serve with the noodles.

The Chinese have been making wine from herbs, leaves, rice, and spices for centuries.

NONYA MEE

Nonya is the name used to describe locally born Chinese people in Malaysia, Malacca, Singapore, and southern Thailand. They have their own customs, dress, and cuisine. This is one of the best-known of their dishes. When you eat in a local restaurant serving Nonya food you will generally find sambal sauce on the table, which you add to suit your own taste.
Serves 4

2 tablespoons vegetable oil
¼ cup finely sliced shallots
3 garlic cloves, finely chopped
1 tablespoon soy sauce
10½ ounces raw medium shrimp, peeled and deveined
3½ cups mustard greens, cut into 1¼-inch pieces
2 cups fresh bean sprouts
1¾ pounds cooked medium egg noodles, rinsed under cold water,
    and drained
scant 1 cup vegetable stock (see page 19)
½ teaspoon salt

To serve
fresh lime juice
sambal ulek (see page 46)

1 Heat the oil in a wok and stir-fry the shallots until golden brown. Remove and set aside.
2 Add the garlic and soy sauce to the oil and cook, stirring, until fragrant. Add the shrimp, mustard greens, and bean sprouts, and cook, stirring lightly, until the shrimp are nearly cooked.
3 Add the noodles, stock, and salt, stir well, and bring to a boil. Simmer for 2 minutes, stirring continuously.
4 Stir in the shallots and serve, adding lime juice and *sambal ulek* to taste.

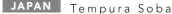

FRIED SHRIMP WITH SOBA NOODLES

Shiitake are a variety of mushroom that grow on wood. Commonly used in Japanese and Chinese cuisine, they are available in both fresh and dried form. If you buy them dried, they will have a more concentrated flavor but must be soaked before use. The soaking liquid can then be used as a tasty stock.

Serves 4

1 egg, beaten
¼ cup all-purpose flour
½ teaspoon chili powder
8 raw large shrimp, peeled and deveined
8 shiitake mushrooms
about 1 cup vegetable oil, for deep-frying
14 ounces soba noodles
1½ quarts Japanese stock (*dashi*—see page 19)

1 In a bowl, lightly mix the egg, 3 tablespoons of the flour, and ½ cup water to make the batter. It should be quite lumpy, with some flour visible on top of the mixture.
2 Coat the shrimp with the remaining flour and chili powder and then dip into the batter, making sure they are completely coated. Dip the mushrooms in the batter.
3 Heat the oil in a wok over high heat, add the shrimp and mushrooms, and deep-fry until golden brown. Remove with a slotted spoon, drain on paper towels, and set aside.
4 Bring a large pan of water to a boil, add the noodles, and cook for 5 minutes, or according to the package directions, then drain and rinse under cold running water. Divide among 4 serving bowls.
5 Pour the stock into a pan and bring to a boil, then pour it over the noodles. Add 2 shrimp and 2 mushrooms to each bowl and serve.

Shiitake

INDONESIAN FRIED NOODLES WITH FISH AND SHRIMP

Sweet soy sauce is a dark soy sauce made from soy sauce, sugar, and malt sugar.
Serves 4

8 tablespoons peanut oil
1 onion, chopped
2 garlic cloves, chopped
1 pound firm white fish fillets, such as cod or halibut, cut into
    1¼-inch pieces
1 celery stalk, finely chopped
2 teaspoons *sambal ulek* (see page 46)
1 tablespoon sweet soy sauce
salt and pepper
2 tablespoons finely chopped chives
¼ pound raw medium shrimp, peeled and deveined
1 teaspoon cornstarch, mixed with 1 tablespoon cold water
2 small red or green chiles, finely chopped
¾ pound rice vermicelli noodles, cooked according to the
    package directions, rinsed under cold water, and drained

1 Heat 3 tablespoons of the oil in a wok and stir-fry the onion until it is transparent, then add the garlic and fish. Sprinkle the celery over the dish, add the *sambal ulek* and ½ cup boiling water, and cook for 1 minute.
2 Add the soy sauce and season with salt and pepper. Stir in the chives, cover the wok, and cook for 4 minutes.
3 Add the shrimp, stir in the cornstarch mixture, and cook, stirring, until the sauce has thickened. Add the chiles, stir briefly, then set aside in a warmed bowl. Wipe out the wok.
4 In the wok, heat the remaining 5 tablespoons oil and stir-fry the noodles for 4 to 5 minutes. Turn into a large warmed serving dish, spoon the sauce over, and serve.

THAI FRIED NOODLES WITH JUMBO SHRIMP

This is Thailand's most famous dish, served everywhere from street vending stalls to smart restaurants. It is mostly cooked with shrimp, but can also be made with pork or chicken instead or as well as the crustaceans.
Serves 4

3 tablespoons peanut oil

2 garlic cloves, finely chopped

16 raw jumbo shrimp, peeled and deveined

¼ pound fried tofu, cut into ½-inch cubes

3 eggs

1 pound medium rice stick noodles, cooked according to
    the package directions, rinsed under cold water, and drained

2 tablespoons finely chopped preserved radish (available at
    Asian markets)

2 tablespoons fish sauce

2 tablespoons light soy sauce

1 tablespoon dark soy sauce

1 tablespoon sugar

3 tablespoons tamarind water (tamarind paste is available at
    Asian markets)

1 tablespoon white wine vinegar

To garnish

½ teaspoon chili powder

4 scallions, finely chopped

1¼ cups fresh bean sprouts

3 tablespoons chopped roasted peanuts

2 limes, quartered

1 Heat the oil in a wok and stir-fry the garlic and shrimp until the shrimp are just cooked.

2 Add the tofu and stir briefly, then add the eggs and stir into the mixture.

3 Add the noodles and stir well, then add all the remaining ingredients, one by one in the above order, stirring well after each addition. Transfer to a platter and serve, mixing in the garnishes to your individual taste.

This is Thailand's most famous dish, served everywhere, from street vending stalls to smart restaurants.

SHANTUNG-STYLE NOODLES

Bunches of fresh or dried egg noodles are sold in Asian food stores and many Western supermarkets as well. They can be kept in a refrigerator or frozen.

Serves 4

1½ quarts vegetable stock (see page 19)

½ pound lean pork, boiled quickly, then cut into thin 1-inch squares

20 raw medium shrimp, peeled and deveined

1 small cucumber, sliced

4 dried wood ear (cloud ear) mushrooms, soaked in warm water for 20 minutes, drained, stems discarded, and cut into 1-inch strips

3 tablespoons light soy sauce

1 teaspoon salt

2 tablespoons cornstarch mixed with cold water to a paste

2 eggs, beaten

½ tablespoon sesame oil

4 bunches egg noodles, cooked according to the package directions, rinsed under cold water, drained, and divided among 4 serving bowls

1 Bring the stock to a boil and add the pork, shrimp, cucumber slices, mushrooms, soy sauce, and salt. Stir in the cornstarch paste, then reduce the heat, add the beaten eggs, and continue to cook, stirring, until the pork and shrimp are cooked through.

2 Turn off the heat and splash the sesame oil on top. Add a generous dollop of the mixture to each portion of noodles and serve.

FRIED NOODLES WITH CRAB AND TOFU

Tofu is a silky, protein-rich substance made from soy milk. It originated in ancient China and nowadays is often used as a meat substitute. Firm tofu comes in blocks or cakes, and may be kept in the refrigerator for a few days after opening.

Serves 4

3 tablespoons vegetable oil

2 garlic cloves, finely chopped

¼ pound firm tofu, fried and cut into ¾-inch cubes

¼ pound lump crabmeat

½ pound rice stick noodles, soaked in warm water for 20 minutes, rinsed under cold water, and drained

1¼ cups fresh bean sprouts

4 scallions, cut into 2-inch lengths

2 tablespoons fish sauce

2 tablespoons light soy sauce

3 tablespoons fresh lime juice

1 teaspoon sugar

2 tablespoons chopped roasted peanuts

½ teaspoon chili powder

1 In a wok, heat the oil and stir-fry the garlic until golden. Add the tofu and crabmeat, and stir well.

2 Add the noodles and then all the remaining ingredients, stirring well for a few moments. Transfer to a warmed platter and serve.

VIETNAMESE SHRIMP, MUSHROOM, AND NOODLE SOUP

I ate this dish at a seaside restaurant at China Beach in Vietnam, and asked the chef f or the recipe.
Serves 4

3½ cups vegetable stock (see page 19)
8 button mushrooms, quartered
2 tablespoons fish sauce
1 teaspoon sugar
6 ounces mung bean vermicelli noodles
½ pound raw medium shrimp, peeled and deveined
2 small cucumbers, peeled and cut into thin sticks

1 Pour the stock into a pan, add the mushrooms, fish sauce, and sugar, and set aside.
2 Soak the noodles for 5 minutes in water that has been boiled and cooled slightly, then drain and divide among 4 serving bowls. Meanwhile, bring the stock and mushroom mixture to a boil, add the shrimp, and simmer until the shrimp are just cooked, 2 minutes.
3 Place the cucumber over the noodles, pour the hot stock, mushroom, and shrimp broth over, and serve.

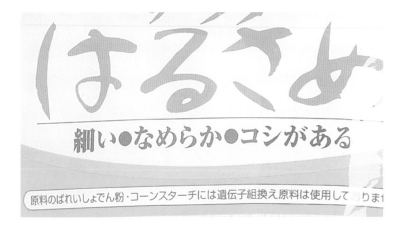

BURMESE NOODLES WITH SHRIMP

Turmeric is native to Southeast Asia and is widely used in the region's cuisine, particularly in Burma. The locals also apply the ground spice externally, as it is thought to improve skin tone.
Serves 4

3 tablespoons peanut oil

⅓ cup coarsely chopped onion

½ pound raw medium shrimp, peeled and deveined

10 ounces rice vermicelli noodles, soaked in warm water for 5 minutes,
    rinsed under cold water, and drained

1 teaspoon ground turmeric

1 teaspoon sugar

2 tablespoons fish sauce

¼ pound tomatoes, cut into wedges

4 scallions, finely chopped

cilantro sprigs, to garnish

1 Heat the oil in a wok, add the onion, and stir-fry briefly, then add the shrimp and stir-fry until almost cooked.

2 Add the noodles and stir quickly, then add all the other ingredients, one by one in the above order, except the cilantro, stirring once after each addition. Transfer to a serving plate, garnish with cilantro sprigs, and serve.

Turmeric is native to Southeast Asia and is used widely in the region's cookery, particularly in Burma, where it is also ground and applied externally, as it is thought to improve skin tone.

VEGETARIAN *Noodles*

When I visit Japan, I am always struck by the contrast of ancient customs with modernity: kimonos and cutting-edge fashion; Shinto temples and ultra-modern architecture. In food, however, there has not been much change, except in the places where it is served. These range from traditional sushi bars to ultra-sleek restaurants where the food passes in front of you on a conveyor belt. Noodle bars likewise vary from the small and wooden to the ultra modern.

In Hong Kong I ate noodles in a smart café on the fiftieth floor and I had a similar experience in Shanghai. There are also modern stylish restaurants of this kind in London and Bangkok. In Los Angeles, Chinatown has been moved from its original location to a new modern area in which food products from all over Asia are available. In the local noodle restaurants, photographs of all the dishes are displayed on the walls, so you don't need to speak the language to order the food. You just point at the relevant photo.

Originally, Asians thought of noodles as a very basic food. In the last twenty years they have undergone a transformation. Noodles are still sold in markets and served at roadside stalls, but they are also on offer in the smartest and most fashionable restaurants. Go back another twenty years and, with a few exceptions, noodle dishes were almost unknown outside Asia. Now they are available everywhere.

One of the most influential developments has been the invention of instant noodles. Originally developed in China centuries ago, where noodles were deep-fried to allow them to be kept for long periods, they were reinvented in Japan in 1971 as pot noodles. Sold in waterproof foam containers, they have become popular all over the world. Available in a huge variety of flavors, including vegetarian ones, they can be mixed with freshly cut cooked meat or fish, and are about as convenient as "convenience food" gets.

Ten Zaru

DEEP-FRIED VEGETABLES AND NOODLES

While traveling around Japan, I noticed many restaurants where there were models of the different dishes outside. This system makes ordering the food very simple.

Serves 4

vegetable oil, for deep-frying

For the batter
1 egg, beaten
²⁄₃ cup all-purpose flour

1 medium eggplant, halved and sliced
4 shiitake mushrooms, stems discarded
1 cup carrots, cut into thin sticks
16 yard-long or green beans, trimmed
14 ounces soba noodles

For the dipping sauce
Japanese stock (*dashi*—see page 19), chilled

1 Heat the vegetable oil for deep-frying in a deep pan over high heat until very hot.
2 Make the batter: place the egg, flour, and 1 cup cold water in a bowl and beat well. Dip the vegetables in the batter, then deep-fry in the hot oil until golden brown. Remove with a slotted spoon and drain on paper towels.
3 Bring a large pan of water to a boil, and cook the noodles for 4 to 6 minutes or according to the package directions. Drain, rinse under cold running water, and then drain again.
4 Divide the noodles among 4 serving bowls. Place the battered vegetables on a serving platter, divide the chilled stock for dipping among 4 small bowls, and serve.

NOODLE SALAD WITH PEANUT SAUCE

Gado-gado is one of Indonesia's most famous dishes, sold everywhere from street hawkers' stalls to the most exclusive restaurants. As you might expect, different areas of the vast Indonesian archipelago have their own versions of the basic recipe.

Serves 4

For the peanut sauce

1 tablespoon vegetable oil
2 garlic cloves, crushed
1 shallot, finely chopped
½ teaspoon chili powder
1 tablespoon sugar
8 tablespoons chunky peanut butter
½ teaspoon salt
2 tablespoons fresh lemon juice

1 cup sliced green cabbage
2 cups fresh bean sprouts
²/3 cup green beans
½ cup carrots cut into thin sticks
14 ounces fresh thin egg noodles
1 tablespoon sesame oil

1 To make the peanut sauce, heat the oil in a wok or large skillet and stir-fry the garlic and shallot for 1 minute. Add the chili powder, 2 cups water, the sugar, and peanut butter, and stir well. Add the salt and lemon juice, stir, and simmer gently to keep warm.

2 Bring a pan of water to a boil and blanch the cabbage, bean sprouts, green beans and carrots for 2 to 3 minutes, then drain.

3 Bring another pan of water to a boil and cook the noodles for 3 minutes or according to the package directions, then rinse under cold running water and drain well. Toss with the sesame oil and divide among 4 serving bowls. Top with the vegetables, pour the peanut sauce over, and serve.

Gado-gado is one of Indonesia's most famous dishes, sold everywhere from street hawkers' stalls to the most exclusive restaurants.

CRISPY NOODLES

This dish is a sweet dish from central Thailand. It is usually eaten with a hot curry to offset the sweetness, but can also be served in small portions as a starter.
Serves 2

1 cup vegetable oil, for deep-frying
6 ounces rice vermicelli noodles

For the sauce
1 tablespoon vegetable oil
2 x 2½-inch square blocks firm tofu,
   cut into ¼-inch cubes
1 medium onion, finely chopped
2 garlic cloves, finely chopped
2 tablespoons soy sauce
2 tablespoons palm sugar
2 tablespoons tamarind water
   (tamarind paste is available at
   Asian markets)

To garnish
1 tablespoon vegetable oil
1 egg, lightly beaten
¾ cup fresh bean sprouts
3 scallions, cut into 1-inch
   slivers
2 medium fresh red chiles,
   seeded and finely sliced
10 pickled garlic cloves, finely
   sliced

1 First cook the vermicelli: heat the oil for deep-frying in a wok over medium heat, add the noodles, and deep-fry until crisp and golden brown. Drain and set aside. Pour off the oil and wipe out the wok.

2 To make the sauce, heat the oil in the wok, add the tofu cubes, and stir-fry until crisp. Remove with a slotted spoon and set aside. Stir-fry the onion and garlic until they are lightly browned. Add the soy sauce, palm sugar, and tamarind water, and cook, stirring, until the mixture begins to caramelize. Add the reserved tofu, stir quickly, and remove from the heat.

3 For the garnish, in a small wok or skillet, heat the the oil and drizzle in the beaten egg to make ribbons of cooked egg. Drain and set aside.

4 Return the sauce to the heat and crumble in the crispy noodles, mixing gently. Turn into a serving dish, sprinkle over the cooked egg, bean sprouts, scallions, chiles, and pickled garlic, and serve.

Wakame Ramen

SEAWEED AND RAMEN NOODLE SOUP

This is a classic Japanese noodle soup. The seaweed is full of beneficial vitamins and minerals, and is virtually calorie-free.
Serves 4

1 pound ramen noodles
1½ quarts vegetable stock (see page 19)
2 tablespoons dried green seaweed (*wakame*), soaked in hot water for
    5 minutes and drained
¼ pound canned, drained sliced bamboo shoots, cut into thin sticks
2 scallions, chopped
2 hard-boiled eggs, shelled and halved

1 Bring a large pan of water to a boil, add the noodles, and cook until tender, about 4 minutes or according to the package directions. Drain and divide among 4 serving bowls.
2 Heat the vegetable stock in a pan. Place the seaweed, bamboo shoots, scallions, and eggs on the noodles, pour the hot stock over, and serve.

JAPAN Kuksu

COLD NOODLES WITH VEGETABLES

Sesame seed is one of the earliest recorded seasonings. To toast, either fry in a dry pan for 3 to 4 minutes or roast in a hot oven for 15 minutes.
Serves 4

3 tablespoons Japanese light soy
    sauce (*shoyu*)
2 teaspoons sugar
1 tablespoon sesame oil
1¼ cups fresh bean sprouts
1 pound fresh spinach leaves,
    stems discarded
2 cups vegetable stock
    (see page 19)

½ pound rice vermicelli noodles
5 dried Chinese black (shiitake)
    mushrooms, soaked in warm
    water for 30 minutes, drained,
    stems discarded, and thinly sliced
2 scallions, diagonally sliced
1 tablespoon toasted sesame seeds

1 In a bowl, mix together 2 tablespoons of the soy sauce, the sugar, and the sesame oil, and set aside.
2 In a pan, bring 2½ cups water to a boil, and blanch the bean sprouts for 10 seconds. Remove with a slotted spoon, rinse under cold running water, and let drain.
3 Add the spinach to the boiling water and blanch until it wilts, then drain, rinse under cold running water, and drain again.
4 Pour the stock into another pan, add the remaining soy sauce, and bring to a boil. Add the noodles and cook until just soft. Remove the noodles from the stock and place in a serving bowl.
5 Add the spinach and mushrooms to the stock, heat through quickly, then remove from the stock and place on the noodles, seasoning with a little of the soy sauce, sugar, and sesame oil mixture.
6 Place the bean sprouts on top of the spinach and mushrooms, pour the stock around the noodles, then garnish with the scallions and sesame seed and serve.

NOODLE SALAD

Made in quantity, this is a very good party dish. It is also excellent for picnics, as you can easily pack and carry it. It is best served with fried chicken wings and cucumber slices.
Serves 6

2 pounds fresh egg noodles
4 tablespoons vegetable oil
I large onion, cut lengthwise and thinly sliced
½ teaspoon ground turmeric
1¼ cups fresh bean sprouts
4 scallions, finely chopped
¼ cup fresh lime juice
3 tablespoons light soy sauce

1 In a pan, bring 1 quart water to a boil, then add the noodles and cook until just tender, 4 to 5 minutes or according to the package directions. Drain, rinse under cold running water, then drain again and set aside.
2 Heat 2 tablespoons of the vegetable oil in a skillet over medium heat, add the onion and turmeric, and cook, stirring, until golden brown. Remove from the heat and set aside.
3 Heat the remaining 2 tablespoons oil in a large wok over medium heat, add the bean sprouts, scallions, noodles, lime juice, and soy sauce, and mix well. Stir in the onion mixture and serve.

JAPAN Kitsune Udon

JAPANESE TOFU NOODLES

Japanese tofu (bean curd) is generally softer, whiter, and more delicately flavored than other kinds. It is sometimes known as cotton bean curd because it is strained through a fine cloth.
Serves 4

1½ pounds fresh udon noodles
6 cups Japanese stock (*dashi*—see page 19)
4 sheets Japanese firm tofu, cut in half
1 tablespoon sugar
2 tablespoons Japanese soy sauce
½ pound spinach leaves, coarsely chopped
2 scallions, finely sliced

1 In a pan, bring 1 quart water to a boil and cook the noodles for 3 minutes or according to the package directions. Drain, rinse under cold running water, then drain again. Divide the noodles among 4 serving bowls.
2 Heat the stock, add the tofu, sugar, and soy sauce, and simmer for 20 minutes.
3 Meanwhile, blanch the spinach in boiling water for 1 minute, then drain and squeeze out the excess water.
4 Place the tofu and spinach over the noodles, then pour over the stock, scatter with the scallions, and serve.

FRIED NOODLES WITH MUSHROOMS AND CHINESE BROCCOLI

Vegetarian food is still gaining in popularity in my country, mainly for reasons of health. Chinese broccoli is also known as Chinese kale or kai-lan.
Serves 4

2 tablespoons vegetable oil

2 garlic cloves, finely chopped

8 dried Chinese black (shiitake) mushrooms, soaked in warm water for 30 minutes, drained, stems discarded, and finely sliced

2 eggs

½ pound rice vermicelli noodles, soaked in warm water for 5 minutes, rinsed under cold water, and drained

3 tablespoons light soy sauce

1 tablespoon dark soy sauce

½ teaspoon ground white pepper

1 teaspoon sugar

½ pound Chinese broccoli, finely sliced

1 Heat the oil in a wok and stir-fry the garlic until golden. Add the mushrooms and stir.

2 Add the eggs to the wok and cook briefly, stirring, then add the noodles and stir well. Add the soy sauces, pepper, and sugar, and stir well again.

3 Finally, add the Chinese broccoli and stir well for a few moments, then turn into a large dish and serve.

Beehoon

VEGETARIAN NOODLES

This is a Chinese Malay dish in the Nonya style. In other words, it is a traditional Chinese dish adapted to suit local tastes.
Serves 4

2 tablespoons vegetable oil
6 garlic cloves, finely chopped
1 large onion, finely sliced
5 long white Chinese (napa) cabbage leaves, shredded
8 dried Chinese black (shiitake) mushrooms, soaked in warm water for 30 minutes, drained, stems discarded, and sliced
10 to 15 button mushrooms, sliced
1 medium carrot, sliced thinly

½ cup vegetable stock (see page 19)
1 pound 2 ounces rice vermicelli noodles, soaked in warm water for 10 minutes, rinsed under cold water, and drained
¼ cup light soy sauce
2 tablespoons dark soy sauce
2 cups fresh bean sprouts
salt and pepper

1 Heat the oil in a wok and stir-fry the garlic until golden brown. Stir in the onion and cabbage, then the mushrooms and carrot. Pour in the stock and cook, stirring, over high heat for 1 minute.

2 Stir in the noodles, mixing well, then add the soy sauces. Cook, stirring, for 1 minute, then add the bean sprouts and mix well. Season with salt and pepper, stir well, and serve.

Nonya Chap Chai

NONYA VEGETARIAN FRIED NOODLES

This recipe uses red pickled tofu, also called "preserved tofu" or "fermented tofu." Sold in jars in most Asian markets, it has a very strong, pungent flavor.
Serves 4

3 tablespoons peanut oil
3 garlic cloves, finely chopped
1 teaspoon red pickled tofu
1 medium onion, thinly sliced
1½ cups coarsely chopped Chinese (napa) cabbage
½ cup coarsely chopped carrots
1 cup fresh wood ear (cloud ear) mushrooms, coarsely chopped
1 cup snow peas, topped and tailed, and strings discarded

10 ounces mung bean vermicelli noodles, soaked in warm water for 10 minutes, rinsed under cold water, and drained
2¼ ounces dried tofu skin (bean curd sheet), broken into small pieces, soaked in warm water for 2 minutes, rinsed under cold water, and drained
3 tablespoons light soy sauce
1 teaspoon sugar
½ teaspoon ground black pepper

1 Heat the oil in a wok, then add all the remaining ingredients, one by one in the above order, stirring once after each addition. After stirring in the pepper, turn into a large dish and serve.

NOODLES WITH PEANUT SAUCE AND VEGETABLES

Sichuan province is known as "the province of abundance," since all types of fruit and vegetables grow easily in its fertile valleys. Sichuan cuisine uses lots of chiles and garlic, and can be described in four words: spicy, hot, fresh, and fragrant.
Serves 4

3 tablespoons chunky peanut butter
1 tablespoon sesame oil
¼ cup vegetable oil
1 pound fresh egg noodles, cooked in boiling water for 1 minute, rinsed briefly under cold water, and drained

4 tablespoons dry-roasted peanuts, lightly crushed
2 scallions, shredded
1¼ cups fresh bean sprouts, blanched in boiling water, rinsed under cold water, and drained
1 small cucumber, diced

1 In a bowl, blend the peanut butter with the sesame oil to form a smooth paste, then set aside.

2 In a wok, heat the vegetable oil and fry the noodles, in 2 or 3 batches, turning so that they are evenly cooked. Remove each batch and keep warm while cooking the remainder.

3 Place the noodles on a large platter, then pour the peanut paste over and mix it into the noodles. Scatter the peanuts and scallions on top, arrange the bean sprouts and cucumber around the noodles, and serve.

STIR-FRIED NOODLES WITH VEGETABLES

This basic stir-fry uses a minimum of ingredients to achieve maximum flavor. The vegetables can be changed to take advantage of local seasonal specialties.
Serves 2

1 tablespoon vegetable oil
2 garlic cloves, finely chopped
1 medium carrot, thinly sliced
1 medium head Chinese (napa) cabbage, shredded
2 celery stalks, grated
3 tablespoons vegetable stock (see page 19)
2 tablespoons light soy sauce

1 teaspoon sugar
1½ teaspoons ground black pepper
½ pound rice vermicelli noodles, soaked in warm water for 5 minutes, rinsed under cold water, and drained
hot chili sauce, to serve

1 Heat the oil in a wok and stir-fry the garlic until golden brown. Add the carrot and stir-fry for 1 minute, then add all the remaining ingredients, except the noodles, with ¼ cup water and cook for 2 minutes, stirring gently.

2 Add the noodles and stir to mix all the ingredients thoroughly. Continue to cook, stirring, for 1 minute, then serve with hot chili sauce.

RICE NOODLES IN SPICY SOUP

This Nonya specialty consists of noodles in a hot sour soup. The salted soybeans and tamarind give this recipe a delightful tang. It is a popular snack at food stalls throughout Singapore.
Serves 4

10 dried red chiles, split, soaked
    in hot water for 5 minutes,
    and drained
6 garlic cloves
3 tablespoons vegetable oil
½ cup dry-roasted peanuts, ground
1 tablespoon sugar
1 tablespoon tamarind water
5½ ounces rice vermicelli noodles,
    soaked in warm water for
    5 minutes, rinsed under cold
    water, and drained

1 cup fresh bean sprouts
2 x 2½-inch squares firm tofu,
    fried and drained on paper towels
2 hard-boiled eggs, shelled and
    cut into wedges
2 scallions, finely sliced
salt and pepper

1 For the sauce, blend the chiles, garlic, and 1 tablespoon of the oil to a paste. In a wok, heat the remaining 2 tablespoons oil and gently fry the paste for 2 minutes.
2 Add the peanuts, sugar, tamarind water, and 3 cups water, then bring to a boil and simmer gently for 5 minutes. Season with salt and pepper.
3 Place 3 tablespoons of the sauce in a wok and stir in the noodles, mixing well.
4 Divide the noodles among 4 serving bowls, add the bean sprouts, tofu, and eggs, then pour over the remaining sauce, garnish with the scallions, and serve.

SWEET AND SOUR NOODLES WITH VEGETABLES

Chinese plum sauce, in which plums are used to give a sweet and sour taste, is often used as a condiment.
Serves 4

½ pound rice vermicelli noodles

2 tablespoons vegetable oil

2 garlic cloves, finely chopped

6 dried Chinese black (shiitake) mushrooms, soaked in warm water for 30 minutes, drained, stems discarded, and finely sliced

1 medium onion, cut into 8 segments, then the layers separated

1 red bell pepper, seeded and cut into thin strips

1 tablespoon peeled and finely shredded fresh ginger

1 cup sliced carrots

1 cup sliced cucumber

1 cup sliced celery

1 cup canned, drained sliced bamboo shoots

2 small red chiles, finely chopped

½ cup fresh or canned, drained sliced pineapple

3 tablespoons light soy sauce

1 tablespoon dark soy sauce

2 tablespoons Chinese rice wine

2 tablespoons Chinese plum sauce

3 tablespoons white wine vinegar

2 tablespoons sugar

1½ cups vegetable stock (see page 19)

1 tablespoon cornstarch

salt and pepper

1 Soak the noodles in warm water for 5 minutes. Rinse under cold running water, drain, and then set aside.

2 Heat the oil in a wok and stir-fry the garlic until golden, then add all the remaining ingredients, one by one in the above order, adding the noodles after the vegetables, stirring well after each addition.

3 Continue cooking, stirring continuously, until the sauce thickens, then season with salt and pepper. Place the noodles on a serving platter, turn the mixture onto the noodles, and serve.

DEEP-FRIED NOODLES WITH MIXED VEGETABLES

This dish is served in Chinese restaurants all over the world under a variety of different names. Being Thai, I've naturally gone with the Thai version!
Serves 4

For the noodles
1 cup vegetable oil, for deep-frying
4 bunches egg noodles

For the mixed vegetables
2 tablespoons vegetable oil
2 garlic cloves, finely chopped
1 cup canned, drained sliced bamboo shoots, cut into thin sticks
1½ cups baby corn, halved lengthways
1 small red bell pepper, seeded and diced
3 scallions, cut into 2-inch lengths
2/3 cup canned, drained straw mushrooms
3 tablespoons light soy sauce
1 tablespoon dark soy sauce
1 teaspoon sugar
½ teaspoon ground white pepper
2 tablespoons cornstarch, mixed with 2/3 cup cold water
cilantro leaves, to garnish

1 For the noodles, in a wok, heat the oil for deep-frying over high heat until very hot and deep-fry the noodles until crisp. Remove with a slotted spoon, drain on paper towels, and divide among 4 serving bowls. Pour off the oil and wipe the pan.
2 For the mixed vegetables, heat the oil in the wok and stir-fry the garlic until golden. Add all the remaining ingredients, except the cilantro, stirring continuously, then pour the mixture over the noodles, garnish with cilantro leaves, and serve.

This dish is served in Chinese restaurants all over the world under a variety of different names.

VERMICELLI NOODLE SALAD

This famous dish is served in most Thai restaurants all over the world.
Serves 4

10 large dried wood ear (cloud ear) mushrooms, soaked in warm water for 20 minutes, drained, stems discarded, and coarsely chopped

½ pound mung bean vermicelli noodles, soaked in warm water for 5 minutes, rinsed under cold water, and drained

1 medium onion, halved and thinly sliced

1 cup carrots, cut into thin sticks

2 large celery stalks, finely sliced

1 small red bell pepper, seeded and cut into thin strips

3 tablespoons light soy sauce

1 teaspoon sugar

3 tablespoons fresh lime juice

2 small red chiles, finely chopped

3 scallions, finely chopped

2 tablespoons chopped roasted peanuts

cilantro leaves, to garnish

1 Heat 4 tablespoons water in a wok, add the mushrooms, and stir well.

2 Add the noodles, then all the remaining ingredients, except the peanuts and cilantro, one by one in the above order, stirring well after each addition.

3 Just before serving, add the peanuts and mix well. Turn the mixture onto a platter, garnish with the cilantro leaves, and serve.

DRIED TOFU SKIN AND VERMICELLI NOODLES

Dried tiger-lily buds (also known as golden needles) are the unopened flowers of day lilies. They have been used in Chinese food and medicine for thousands of years.
Serves 4 to 6

½ ounce dried tofu skin (beancurd sheet), soaked in hot water for 30 minutes, drained, and cut into small pieces

1 ounce dried tiger-lily buds (a Chinese ingredient, available online), soaked in hot water for 20 minutes and drained

⅓ cup (¼ ounce) dried wood ear (cloud ear) mushrooms, soaked in water for 20 minutes, drained, stems discarded, and finely sliced

1 pound mung bean vermicelli noodles, soaked according to the package directions until tender, drained, and cut into short lengths

1 teaspoon salt

2 tablespoons light soy sauce

1 tablespoon Chinese rice wine

1 teaspoon peeled and finely chopped fresh ginger

2 scallions, finely chopped

2 teaspoons sesame oil

cilantro leaves, to garnish

1 In a large pan, bring 1 quart water to a boil, add all the remaining ingredients, except the sesame oil and the cilantro, and stir until well bended.

2 Cook for another minute. Stir in the sesame oil, garnish with cilantro leaves, and serve.

TOFU AND EGG NOODLE OMELET

In Indonesia, many side dishes and condiments are served with meals to add or complement flavors. These dishes are known collectively as sambals.

Serves 4

3 tablespoons Indonesian sweet soy sauce
1 tablespoon brown sugar
1 garlic clove, crushed
2 tablespoons *sambal ulek* (see page 46)
1 tablespoon fresh lemon juice
salt and pepper

3 eggs
¼ pound firm tofu
2 scallions, finely chopped
2 teaspoons vegetable oil
½ pound egg noodles, cooked according to the package directions, rinsed under cold water, and drained

1 For the sauce, in a small pan, bring 6 tablespoons water to a boil, add the sweet soy sauce, sugar, and garlic, stir well, and simmer for a few minutes until the mixture is reduced by half. Remove the pan from the heat and let cool slightly.

2 Stir in the *sambal ulek*, lemon juice, and a pinch of salt, then place over very low heat to keep the mixture warm.

3 To make the omelet, break the eggs into a bowl and beat. Crumble the tofu into the eggs, add the scallions and a pinch of salt and pepper, then set aside.

4 In a skillet, heat the oil over high heat, reduce the heat to medium, and add the egg mixture and the cooked noodles to form an omelet. Turn it regularly.

5 While it is still moist, remove the pan from the heat, turn the omelet onto a warmed plate, and fold in half, then pour the sauce mixture over and serve.

In Indonesia, many side dishes and condiments are served with meals to add or complement flavors. These dishes are known collectively as sambals.

STIR-FRIED TOFU AND MIXED VEGETABLES WITH NOODLES

Sambal ulek is a Malaysian spicy chile paste, and there are a number of regional variations. You can increase or decrease the amount according to your preference.
Serves 4

2 x 4-inch square blocks firm tofu

2 cups green beans, cut into ½-inch pieces

5 small young carrots, cut into thin sticks

½ pound broccoli florets

1 medium red bell pepper, seeded and cut into thin strips

2 small green chiles, seeded and cut into thin strips

1¼ cups fresh bean sprouts

3 tablespoons vegetable oil

2 garlic cloves, chopped

1 medium onion, finely chopped

1 teaspoon *sambal ulek* (see page 46)

1 teaspoon sweet soy sauce

½ teaspoon salt

4 to 6 bunches egg noodles, cooked according to the package directions, drained, and tossed in 2 tablespoons sesame oil

1 Cut the tofu into 2-inch x ½-inch strips and set aside.

2 Bring 1½ quarts water to a boil, add the beans, and cook for 2 to 3 minutes. Add the carrots, broccoli florets, bell pepper, and chiles, boil for 5 minutes, then drain.

3 Rinse the bean sprouts in cold water, removing as many seed pods as possible, then drain.

4 Heat the vegetable oil in a wok and stir-fry the garlic until golden brown. Remove with a slotted spoon, drain on paper towels, and set aside. Add the onion to the wok and stir in the *sambal ulek*. Add the tofu and stir well, then sprinkle on the soy sauce and immediately add the cooked vegetables.

5 Add the salt, bean sprouts, and fried garlic, turning carefully until warmed through, then spoon over the noodles in a dish and serve.

You can increase or decrease the amount of sambal you use according to your preference.

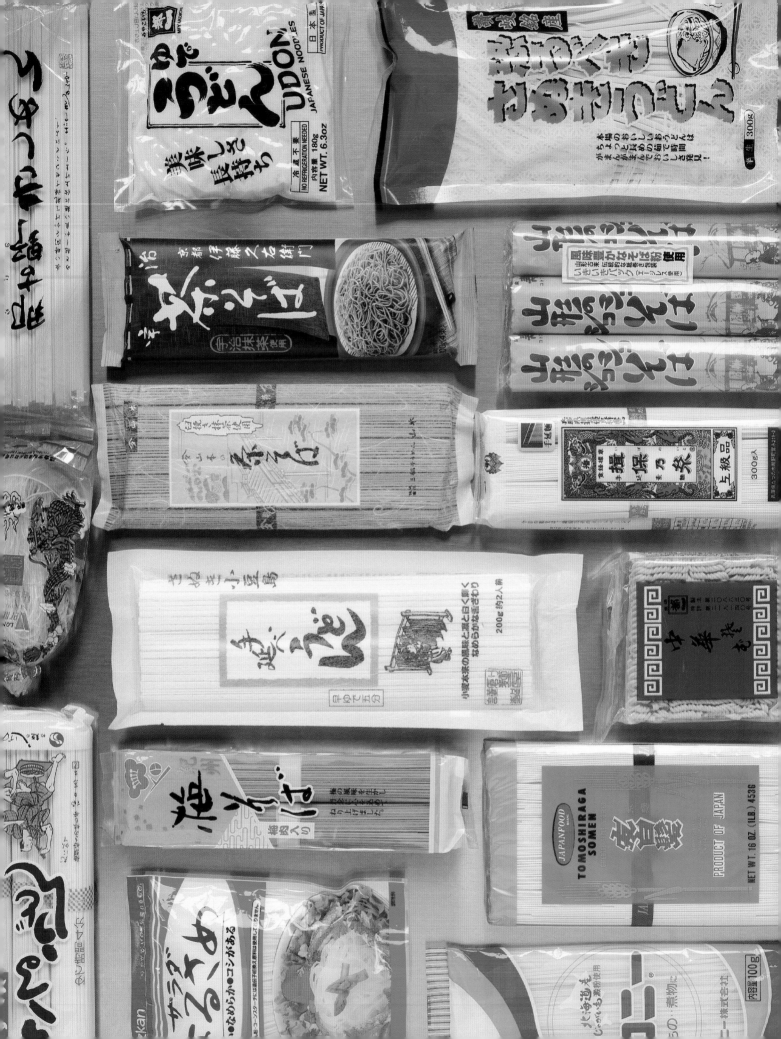

CONVERSION CHART

WEIGHT (SOLIDS)

7g	¼oz
10g	½oz
20g	¾oz
25g	1oz
40g	1½oz
50g	2oz
60g	2½oz
75g	3oz
100g	3½oz
110g	4oz (¼lb)
125g	4½oz
150g	5½oz
175g	6oz
200g	7oz
225g	8oz (½lb)
250g	9oz
275g	10oz
300g	10½oz
310g	11oz
325g	11½oz
350g	12oz (¾lb)
375g	13oz
400g	14oz
425g	15oz
450g	1lb
500g (½kg)	18oz
600g	1¼lb
700g	1½lb
750g	1lb 10oz
900g	2lb
1kg	2¼lb
1.1kg	2½lb
1.2kg	2lb 12oz
1.3kg	3lb
1.5kg	3lb 5oz
1.6kg	3½lb
1.8kg	4lb
2kg	4lb 8oz
2.25kg	5lb
2.5kg	5lb 8oz
3kg	6lb 8oz

VOLUME (LIQUIDS)

5ml	1 teaspoon
10ml	2 teaspoons
15ml	1 tablespoon or ½fl oz
30ml	1fl oz
40ml	1½fl oz
50ml	2fl oz
60ml	2½fl oz
75ml	3fl oz
100ml	3½fl oz
125ml	4fl oz
150ml	5fl oz (¼ pint)
160ml	5½fl oz
175ml	6fl oz
200ml	7fl oz
225ml	8fl oz
250ml (0.25 litre)	9fl oz
300ml	10fl oz (½ pint)
325ml	11fl oz
350ml	12fl oz
370ml	13fl oz
400ml	14fl oz
425ml	15fl oz (¾ pint)
450ml	16fl oz
500ml (0.5 litre)	18fl oz
550ml	19fl oz
600ml	20fl oz (1 pint)
700ml	1¼ pints
850ml	1½ pints
1 liter	1¾ pints
1.2 liters	2 pints
1.5 liters	2½ pints
1.8 liters	3 pints
2 liters	3½ pints

LENGTH

5mm	¼ inch
1cm	¼ inch
2cm	¾ inch
2.5cm	1 inch
3cm	1¼ inches
4cm	1½ inches
5cm	2 inches
7.5 cm	3 inches
10cm	4 inches
15cm	6 inches
18cm	7 inches
20cm	8 inches
24cm	10 inches
28cm	11 inches
30 cm	12 inches

OVEN TEMPERATURES

Celsius*/Farenheit	Gas Mark	Description
110°C/225°F	¼	cool
120°C/250°F	½	cool
130°C/275°F	1	very low
150°C/300°F	2	very low
160°C/325°F	3	low
180°C/350°F	4	moderate
190°C/375°F	5	moderate hot
200°C/400°F	6	hot
220°C/425°F	7	hot
230°C/450°F	8	very hot
240°C/475°F	9	very hot

* For fan-assisted ovens, reduce temperatures by 10°C